LESLIE LINSLEY

First Steps In Counted Cross Stitch

Leslie Linsley Books in This Series:

First Steps in Quilting
First Steps in Stenciling
First Steps in Counted Cross Stitch

LESLIE LINSLEY

First Steps In Counted Cross Stitch

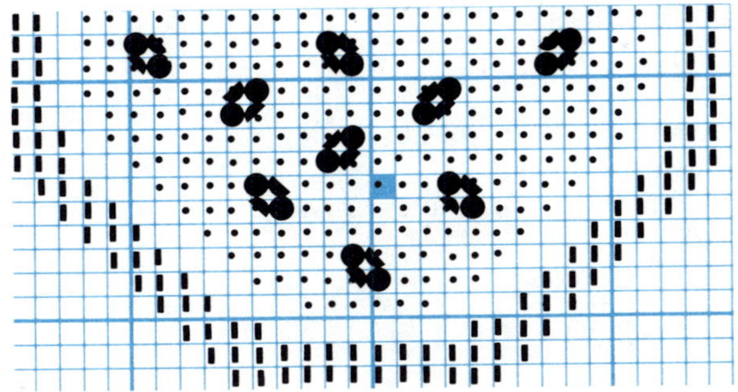

Photography by Jon Aron

Doubleday & Company, Inc., Garden City, New York
1987

Credits

Project Design Director: Jon Aron
Designer and Project Coordinator: Robby Smith
Illustrator: Peter Peluso, Jr.
Crafters: Suzi Peterson
Amy Brunhuber
Ruth Linsley

Special thanks to Suzi Peterson for her excellent craftwork on a major portion of this book.

Library of Congress Cataloging-in-Publication Data

Linsley, Leslie.
First steps in counted cross stitch.

1. Cross stitch—Patterns. I. Title.
TT778.C76L57 1987 746.44 86-16719
ISBN 0-385-19882-5
ISBN 0-385-24100-3 (pbk)

Printed in the United States of America
First Edition

CONTENTS

INTRODUCTION

Counted cross stitch is not a new form of embroidery, but it has always been the most popular. Perhaps this is because it is so easy and always looks perfect. It is possible, for example, to create an illustration with floss and fabric without any training at all.

I was introduced to this craft by my husband, Jon Aron. We have collaborated on many craft books, and that winter, living on Nantucket, we were designing projects for a book of Christmas ornaments and stockings. Jon, who is a graphic designer, was fascinated with charting various designs for stitching. Before long, everyone who came to visit joined us in the den next to the fire to cross stitch. We felt as though we were living as the earliest settlers in this country had. The lanterns outdoors along our cobblestoned street reminded us of bygone days, and on foggy nights the rhythmic sound of the foghorn could be heard in the distance. The church bells chiming the hours made everything even more magical than I'm sure it was two hundred years ago. Thus the craft of cross stitching began in our household and has continued in our apartment in New York City, my mother's home in Florida, my daughter's home in Connecticut, and it will probably continue into her children's homes. I'm sure that years from now my grandchildren, if I have them, will find all the projects that have survived through the years and we will happily remember the good times we had making them. The projects that we've created represent a modern interpretation of the craft in terms of design. Perhaps, just as an early sampler looks charmingly old to us, our cross stitched pillows and framed illustrations will look equally charming, in their own way, to the generations that follow.

Counted cross stitch is basically simple. You need a blunt embroidery needle, a hoop to hold the even-weave fabric made especially for this craft and a charted design. The fabric looks like little squares, and each square is filled in with an X stitch in the color indicated on the chart. Perhaps you have seen early American samplers dating back to Colonial days. Often cross stitches were used to create the neat geometric rows that formed patterns, borders, numbers, letters and sometimes scenes. Originating in Europe, cross stitch was adapted by our early settlers and is now part of our American folk art heritage. Today's renewed interest has fostered a modern approach to the craft, and we find almost every design imaginable, from familiar storybook characters to sayings such as Keep This Kitchen Clean . . . Eat Out. However, the traditional designs, such as flowers, samplers and country motifs adapted from American folk art and quilts, seem to be the most sought after, perhaps because the stitching of a traditional motif allows us to carry on a crafting tradition begun early in this country.

Counted cross stitch is inexpensive to produce; the materials are few and one can do it in odd moments of relaxation. The work-in-progress can fit easily into a purse, and the design possibilities are endless. Add to this a guarantee for a perfectly finished project and you have the ideal leisure time craft. There are designs that fit any occasion, which makes this a wonderful way to give something handmade. For example, it seems that every week someone I know is having a baby. A framed counted cross stitch scene or a tiny decorative pillow is just the thing, and the gift certainly won't be duplicated. For the holidays, whip up some ornaments, door decoration or a special stocking, all of which will last forever and make each successive holiday all the more special.

Materials for Counted Cross Stitch

Design:

This is the most important element in counted cross stitch. Without a design, you cannot begin. It's the design that attracts most of us to do a project. A counted cross stitch design is charted on a graph. Each square of the graph represents a square on the fabric. Therefore, to determine where the stitches will be placed, you simply count each row on the graph where a symbol has been placed to indicate the color of that stitch.

Some crafters like to make their own pattern or design, in which case you will need graph paper and colored pencils. Graph paper comes in many sizes. Most of the projects in this book have been designed for 11- or 14-count even-weave fabrics that are most readily available. This means there are 11 or 14 squares to the inch.

Colored pencils are used for charting the designs so that you can see what the finished project will look like. When you are using the designs that are provided here with each project, you can change the colors if so desired. To see what the design will look like in different colors, simply trace the charted design and fill in your own colors for each square of the design.

The more intricate a design, the more time consuming it will be. Sometimes a small design can be deceiving. If there are many color changes throughout the pattern, for example, the project will take more time than you might think. If the background is completely filled with stitches, it will take more time to finish than one in which the background color is simply fabric. As you begin to do some projects, you'll be able to judge this more accurately.

Fabric:

It's important to buy an adequate amount of fabric to make your chosen design. You will need plenty of room all around the design so that it will fit in an embroidery hoop, and can be held comfortably while working, and, if it is appropriate to the project, can be matted and framed.

There are four basic even-weave fabrics made especially for counted cross stitch.

Hardanger is a very tight, small, even-weave fabric that comes 22 squares to the inch. This is used for very small stitches using only 1 strand of embroidery thread. It is similar to petit point when finished. Since it is time consuming to work a design on this fabric, one requires very good eyes and often a magnifying glass as part of the equipment. Since this is an introductory course in the craft of cross stitch, I have avoided using Hardanger for any of the projects.

Aida cloth is the most commonly used even-weave fabric for counted cross stitch. It comes 18, 14 and 11 squares to the inch. The 18 is not often recommended and is therefore not readily available in craft supply stores. I have used 14 and 11 exclusively throughout the book. They are interchangeable, as you can use either for any project. The 14-inch size will produce a smaller version of the same design done on 11 count, and vice versa. Therefore, if the design shown recommends one or the other and gives the dimensions of the finished size, you can easily figure out the difference in size by substituting the other fabric. I prefer the 11 count, as it goes faster. Suzi Peterson, one of our expert craft workers, likes the 14 count because she thinks the finished work is much neater looking.

Aida cloth is most commonly sold in packages of one 12 × 18–inch piece per package. It is 100 percent cotton and therefore is washable. It comes in many colors, but white and ecru seem to be the most popular. You can also purchase prepackaged baby bibs made from Aida cloth with various colored bindings. There are also premade pillows complete with lace and cloth ruffles, with a round or square center area made of Aida cloth for applying your cross stitch design. Recently on the market is a line of pillow squares that are printed with a border design in color. You simply apply your design in the center and then finish the pillow with your own trimmings.

Gingham and other *checked fabric* can also be used for counted cross stitch. Each check on the fabric is equal to one check on the charted design that you are following. Since this fabric comes in many different sizes, you have the option of choosing the size of your pattern from one that is very tiny to quite a large design. Avoid buying checked fabric that is too large, because if your stitches are very large, you lose the tautness that gives a design definition. It is the closeness of the stitches that fills each square with color in order to create the design.

Penelope cloth is sometimes used by experienced crafters but is not included for any of the projects in this book. However, for your further information, it is a canvas that is basted to the fabric you are using for your design. All the threads of the canvas and your fabric must match horizontally and vertically. You work the design by taking diagonal stitches over the double layer of canvas and background fabric without catching the top layer of canvas.

Once the design is completed, you carefully pull each strand of the canvas away in both directions, leaving the finished cross stitch design on the fabric. Now you can see why this particular fabric is not used for a beginner's look on this exciting craft. There is too much room for error and frustration. And there is no satisfaction in projects that have not been completed. This happens all too often when a craft becomes more complicated than it need be.

Fiddler's cloth: This is a little heavier cloth than Hardanger and Aida and feels like burlap. It comes in different sizes and is sold in craft shops, as are the other cloths.

Perforated paper is often used for making such items as greeting cards, napkin rings, small candy or potpourri baskets. It is quite sturdy, and you work with floss as you do on Aida cloth. Perforated paper is available in craft stores or through mail order sources (see p. 16).

Embroidery hoop:

Hoops come in various sizes and styles and are used to hold the fabric taut as you work the embroidery stitches. They are relatively inexpensive and are available in notions stores, five-and-tens and craft shops. Since cross stitch has become so popular, there is a line of plastic snap-together hoops that have been designed to serve as the frame for the finished project. They have a decorative ring on top for hanging and come in a variety of colors in round and oval shapes.

Each time you put your work aside, it's a good idea to remove the fabric from the hoop.

This way you won't form a permanent crease in the fabric. Once the work is finished, you will block and steam the fabric.

Embroidery floss:

A skein of floss is made up of six strands of thread. You will be instructed as to the number of strands to use for each project. The number of strands used together is determined by the fabric used.

Embroidery floss comes in the widest range of colors and shades imaginable. Floss is available in cotton, rayon or silk, but most cross stitch projects use the cotton thread. Along with the list of colors and symbols for each project, I have listed the DMC number of the floss. In this way you can duplicate the exact color in each project if desired. However, since the general color is listed, for example, light blue, you will be able to substitute another brand of floss if necessary. In addition to DMC, you will find floss manufactured by Coats & Clark and Susan Bates, among others.

Needles:

A blunt-end tapestry or embroidery needle is best for cross stitch. It will not catch or ravel the fabric the way a sharply pointed needle might. Be sure that the eye is large enough to receive all six strands of floss, but not so large as to make big holes in the fabric as it passes through.

Embroidery scissors:

These sharp little snipping scissors are invaluable. Keep them next to you while you work. Each time you finish a length of floss, you'll have them handy for snipping. They can also be used for trimming excess fabric around an embroidery hoop frame when it's necessary to cut close.

Ruler:

This is essential, as you will be measuring everything you make in counted cross stitch.

Masking tape:

Used to keep the edges of your fabric from unraveling while the work is in progress. Using 1-inch tape, simply fold it over the edges approximately 1/2 inch on each side. When the work is finished, the tape is easily removed.

Fusible backing:

This is often fused to the back of a design if, for example, you will be cutting it out. To make a coaster that is round, you would work the design on your square piece of Aida cloth and then iron a piece of fusible webbing to the back. Draw your circle on the front of the fabric and cut out. The fusible backing stiffens and gives the fabric body. It is especially useful for making greeting cards and three-dimensional shapes or ornaments. It also helps to block a design for framing and matting.

Matte boards:

If you make a project that is suitable for framing, you might want to surround it with a matte board in one of the colors of the design. Sometimes the frame comes with just the right size and color matting, but more likely you'll want to customize your project with your own color choice.

Mattes are sold in a variety of colors and sizes to fit any standard-size frame. They are available in camera or framing shops. You can also make your own matte boards and even cover them with pretty printed paper or fabric.

Frames:

Preassembled frames come in many sizes and colors as well as styles. I have purchased frames in art supply stores, camera shops, five-and-ten-cent stores and second-hand stores. Always take your finished cross stitch with you when choosing a frame.

How to Work Counted Cross Stitch

Preparing the work:

Each project will tell you the fabric count to use. For example, #14 count Aida means there are 14 squares to the inch. You will also find the fabric color and overall size of the project. Begin by removing the creases from the fabric with a steam iron. Next, bind all raw edges with masking tape so they won't unravel.

Threading the needle:

Each project will list the number of strands of floss required. Begin by cutting an 18-inch length of floss. Separate all six strands and then join the number needed for the project you have chosen. If all six are required, it's still a good idea to separate the strands and rejoin all of them. This keeps the floss from knotting and tangling. When you are using three or more strands, double it around the eye of the needle, holding it taut and as close to the needle as possible. Slide the folded end off the needle while holding it tight. Slip the folded end through the needle eye.

Finding the center:

Find the center of the charted design in the book. Fold the fabric in half horizontally and vertically to find the center of the fabric. Some stitchers like to start their work at this point, but everyone in our studio agrees that it's better to start at the top of the design. Once you've located the center of the design, count up to the top row and out to the first X to find your starting point. Do the same on your fabric. Each square on the charted design represents a corresponding square on the fabric. You are now ready to begin working your stitches in horizontal rows.

Securing the work:

The cross stitch is worked one section at a time. The area is defined within the embroidery hoop. Secure the fabric in the hoop. Tighten the hoop so the fabric is as taut as possible. This makes it easier to insert the needle into the fabric holes, and the stitches will be consistently neat. Even tension produces beautifully perfect work.

Beginning a stitch:

Do not make a knot on one end of the floss as you would for regular sewing. Locate the first square and insert your needle into one fabric hole from the underside. Pull it through until you have a 2-inch tail remaining on the underside. This tail will be secured under the first few stitches after you have finished the work. Reinsert the needle through the hole diagonally to the right, across the first square on the front of the fabric. Continue to do this, working diagonally across the row, using the same color as indicated on the chart.

Cross stitching the design:

When you have completed a section of slanted left to right stitches, cross back to make each stitch into an X. Each time you run out of floss, weave the last bit under a few stitches on the underside to secure the work.

If you are working on an area that has few stitches in each row, you might prefer to

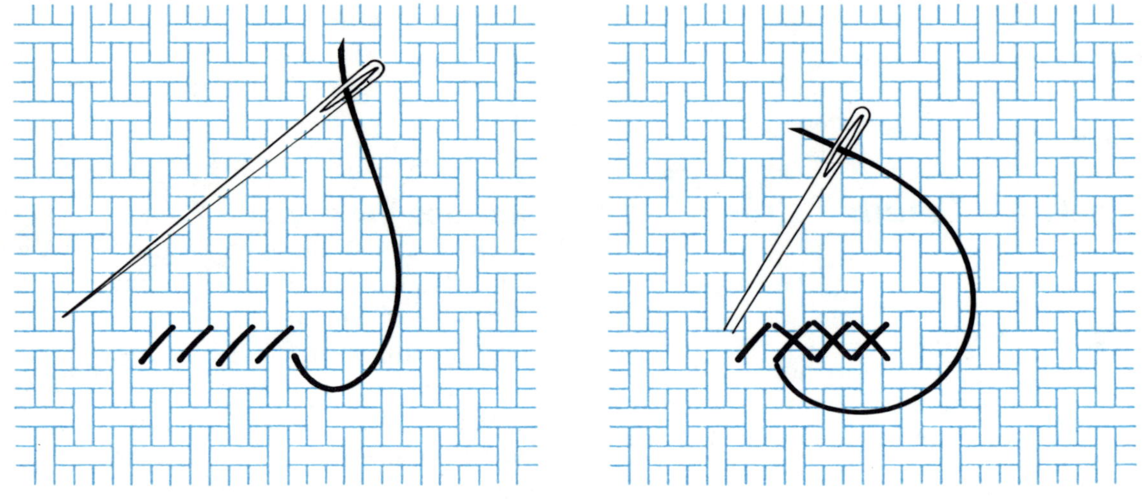

Making a cross stitch

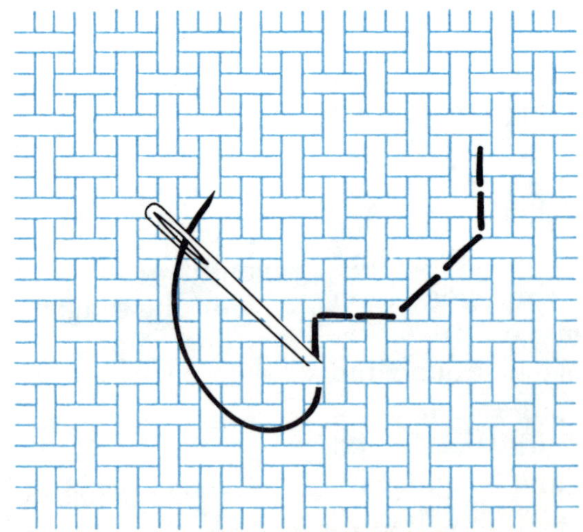

The backstitch

cross each stitch as you work it. With this method you have to make sure each stitch is crossed in the same direction so that the finished work looks neat.

Each hole is worked twice when the stitches are together with no spaces between. When working on isolated stitches, always complete each stitch, end the thread and move to the next area.

Backstitch:

Used for outlining, this stitch looks very much like machine stitching. Stitches are even and close together and often used for stitching sayings on a sampler, for example. Bring the needle up from the underside of the fabric and reinsert it a half stitch behind where the thread came through. Bring it back up a half stitch in front of this point. Continue in this way as indicated on the graph for the cross stitch projects.

Changing color:

When you are beginning a new color, weave the floss under a few stitches on the underside of the fabric and then poke up through the appropriate hole to begin the first stitch. Do not carry one color across an area of fabric that is more than a few stitches, as it will show through to the front. Simply end the floss by weaving under a few stitches, snip and begin again.

Blocking the finished work:

Remove the tape from all edges. Place a terry cloth towel on your ironing board and put the cross stitch piece right side down over the towel. Place a damp cloth on the back of the work and steam-press it.

Mounting the projects:

There are many ways to mount the finished cross stitch. You can use a wooden embroidery hoop, perhaps adding a fabric or eyelet ruffle all around. You can stretch it over artist's stretchers and staple the raw edges to the back of the frame. The most popular way to display cross stitch is in a frame. If your fabric fits the size of a standard frame, you can buy one complete with matte board. The following steps will show you how to mount your fabric for framing.

1. Mark the length and width of the cross stitch piece on cardboard backing, adding extra inches all around for folding the fabric over the edges of the backing.
2. If you want batting between the backing and fabric to add padding, cut a piece of batting 1/8 inch smaller than the cardboard backing all around.
3. Tape or glue (just a few drops here and there) the batting to the backing board.
4. Place the cross stitch face down and center the backing over it with the batting between.
5. Beginning with the centers of each side, pull the fabric tautly over the edges to the back of the board and tape securely.
6. Continue to tape each end of each side in this way until the fabric is tightly secured all around. As you do this, check the right side to be sure the design isn't being pulled so it is distorted.
7. Place the frame over the front of the mounted work and secure in the back with tacks provided with the frame.

The framed work might be matted or bordered with pretty fabric. If a fabric border is added, leave enough seam allowance when cutting the cross stitch fabric for mounting and plan the backing to include the border. The projects in the book that have a fabric border will provide the directions for this.

Tips:

Making errors, missing stitches, finding a letter inappropriately spaced, adding a row where one wasn't called for, leaving stitches unfinished—these are just some of the bothersome things that cross stitchers put up with. To avoid some or all of these, stop to check the stitch placements now and then.

When you are working a border, check often to be sure each corner is going to meet as planned. Fill in the details last, if possible. When you are working on a saying, check to be sure each letter starts and ends on the same row, if that's what is intended.

Before starting a new row, check to be sure all slants are leaning in the same direction. Try to be as consistent in your stitching pattern as possible. If it becomes necessary to remove stitches, it's easier when you don't have an erratic pattern to pull out.

And last, good lighting and a neck-hung magnifying glass will add years to the health of your eyes.

Designing Your Own Cross Stitch

If you'd like to design your own projects, it's easy enough to do. I've provided a variety of borders, designs and alphabets that are interchangeable. For example, you might want to add a border to one of the project designs. Or you might want to add an extra border to an existing project, or change it altogether. You can change the colors that I've used for each project. To see how this will look, use graph paper and colored pencils or markers and a ruler. Copy each square of my design onto your graph in the color of your choice. In this way you can see what the finished design will look like before actually doing the stitching.

Alphabets are provided for many uses. Choose the style that suits you and your design and work it into the project. For example, you might want to make a cross stitch pillow. Use one of the border designs with initials or one initial or a name in the center. Always count the number of squares on the chart and the number of squares on your fabric to be sure the design will fit the area. When working out the borders, take careful measurements so that the squares on the chart match the number of squares per inch on the fabric. You can mix and match designs as well. For example, you might like to use a border design but would like to add the decoration from another border design. Simply chart the border on your graph paper and add the decoration square by square, integrating it into the border. If necessary, eliminate parts of a design where necessary to make it fit. This isn't always possible, but with practice you'll be able to adjust and customize almost any design to suit your taste.

Where to Find It

The best thing about counted cross stitch is that the materials are readily available and inexpensive. The even-weave fabric, embroidery floss, hoops and needles can be found in all five-and-ten-cent stores as well as craft shops. The Gallery frames and mattes used for all framed projects are carried in art supply stores. Here you will also find self-adhesive mounting boards, graph paper for charting your own designs and backing boards for framing.

The premade items such as bibs, place mats and pillow shams made of Aida cloth are also available where other craft materials are sold. The plaid 15 × 15–inch colored fabric pieces are called *Hopscotch* and are made by Charles Craft, Inc. They are distributed to craft outlets nationwide. Some other premade objects ready for cross stitching are coasters, trays, wooden boxes, photo albums, canning jars, pin cushions and key rings, to name a few. These objects have an area of Aida cloth for stitching the decorative designs to enhance the finished item. In this way you can stitch a small design on a round piece of cloth, for example, and insert it into a plastic coaster to finish the project in minutes.

Ruffles, eyelet, piping and other trimmings that will enhance your finished cross stitch projects are available at sewing centers.

If you have trouble finding something or want to share a crafting experience, please drop me a note.

Leslie Linsley
Nantucket, MA 02554

PLATE 1 Little Critters with Daisy Chain, Baby Bag

PLATE 2 Little Jack Horner, Miniature Hang-ups

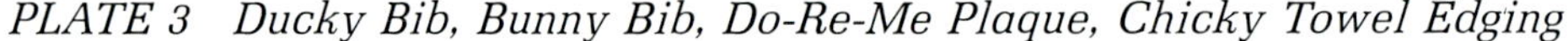

PLATE 3 Ducky Bib, Bunny Bib, Do-Re-Me Plaque, Chicky Towel Edging

PLATE 4 Birth Announcement Sampler, Monogram Pillow, Miniature Hang-ups

PLATE 5 *Mary Had a Little Lamb,*
Shhhh Pillow,
First Day of Spring Pillow,
"Baby Sleeping" Door Hanger

PLATE 6 *Choo-Choo*
Birth Announcement,
ABC Baby Pillow,
Girl in a Swing

Book One

First Steps in Counted Cross Stitch

Just for Baby

MONOGRAM PILLOW

Make a sweet and simple monogrammed pillow for a newborn baby. This project is perfect for a sachet as well. Fill it with sweet-smelling potpourri and edge it with piping rather than a double layer of ruffles. This is a nice gift for any occasion and can be hung in a closet or tucked into a drawer.

The monogram and border designs are worked in pink. You can use the color of your choice, or you might consider making the monogram one color, with each surrounding border in a second color or even multiple colors. The finished size is 10 × 10 inches with the 2-inch ruffle. The Aida pillow is 6 × 6 inches.

Materials

11-count white Aida cloth, 7 × 7 inches
embroidery floss in colors indicated on chart
needle
hoop
strip of pink calico 3½ × 36 inches (can be pieced)
strip of white dotted Swiss or eyelet 2½ × 36 inches (can be pieced)
pink calico, 7 × 7 inches, for backing
polyester stuffing
masking tape

Directions

1. Begin by binding all raw edges of the Aida cloth with masking tape.
2. Using the charted design provided, find the center square, which is solid.
3. Count the number of squares up and out from that point to the beginning of the first line of the charted design.
4. Find the center of the fabric by folding it in half vertically, then horizontally.
5. Each square on the graph corresponds to a square on your fabric. Since they are not always the same size, you count but do not measure.
6. Find your starting point for the first stitch.

To work the stitches

1. Separate the strands of embroidery floss.
2. Rejoin three strands of floss, approximately 18 inches long, and thread your needle.
3. With the Aida secured in the embroidery hoop, begin stitching the pink outside border.
4. Continue to fill in the stitches for each border as indicated on the chart. Check your work often to be sure your corners will meet and that you haven't miscounted.
5. Locate the center of your fabric and count up and out the same number of squares from the center of the graph in order to stitch the letter. Remove tape from edges.
6. When finished, place the work face down on a padded ironing board and steam press.

MONOGRAM PILLOW	Color key	DMC #
	Pink	894

Each square equals 1 stitch

To assemble pillow top

1. With right sides facing and raw edges aligned, stitch together the short ends of the calico strip.
2. Turn one raw edge under 1/4 inch and press.
3. Turn under another 1/4 inch, press and stitch.
4. Divide the fabric into four equal parts and mark with a pin.
5. With right sides facing and raw edges aligned, take small tucks in the fabric as you pin it between these points from corner to corner around the pillow top.
6. Machine stitch all around, leaving a 1/4-inch seam allowance.
7. Hem one long raw edge of the white fabric strip and join short ends to form a loop.
8. Divide into four parts as before and pin to the pillow top as you did the calico strip.
9. From the wrong side, machine stitch the white ruffle to the pillow, leaving a 1/4-inch seam allowance.

To finish pillow

1. With right sides facing and raw edges aligned, pin the backing fabric to the pillow top. The ruffles are between.
2. From the wrong side, machine stitch the backing to the pillow, using the ruffle stitches as a guide. Stitch around three sides and four corners.
3. Trim the corners.
4. Turn the pillow right side out and press from the back side, not over the cross stitch. Press the ruffles all around.
5. Stuff the pillow and slipstitch the opening closed.

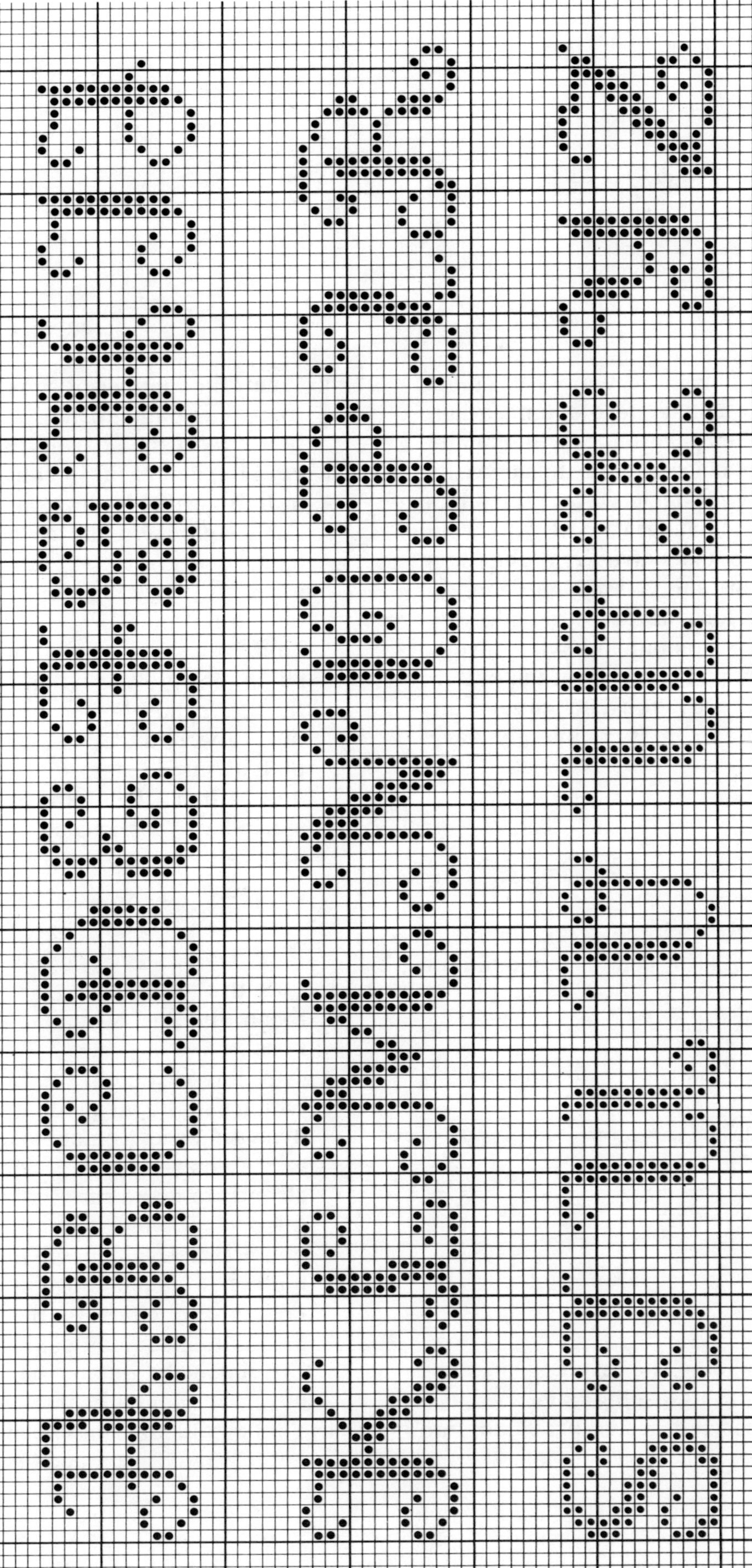

DUCKY BIB

The Aida cloth comes in a variety of colors. This means that unlike needlepoint, where you must fill in the background, with counted cross stitch your colored cloth becomes the background for your design. The pretty blue color serves as the background of water, and you simply stitch the waves and the three ducks. Add a name and you have a delightful personalized gift for your favorite child.

These bibs are premade in white. Make your own quickly and easily with the pattern provided. In this way you can choose any color Aida cloth. The bib is completely washable.

Materials

14-count blue Aida cloth 9 × 11 inches
embroidery floss in colors indicated on chart
needle
hoop
package of double-fold 1-inch-wide bias binding
9 × 11–inch vinyl for backing (optional)
masking tape
tracing paper

Directions

1. Begin by binding all raw edges of the Aida cloth with masking tape.
2. Using the charted design provided, find the center square, which is solid.
3. Count the number of squares up and out from that point to the beginning of the first line of the charted design.
4. Find the center of the fabric by folding it in half vertically, then horizontally.
5. Each square on the graph corresponds to a square on your fabric. Since they are not always the same size, you count but do not measure.
6. Find your starting point for the first stitch. Be sure you will have enough fabric above the design for cutting out the bib pattern once the stitching is complete. You will start with the center duck and stitch the baby ducks, evenly spaced on either side, last. After this you will add the waves and letters.

To work the stitches

1. Separate the strands of embroidery floss.
2. The thread count of the cloth is 14, which usually means that two strands of floss are used. Sometimes, when placing white over a dark color, I use three strands to make sure that each square is filled. Try a few stitches to see which you prefer. Use a length of floss approximately 18 inches long.
3. Follow the chart to determine where each stitch in each color is placed. You can finish the details such as the black eyes and yellow beaks last.
4. Though this design was made for a little boy named Timmy, you can personalize

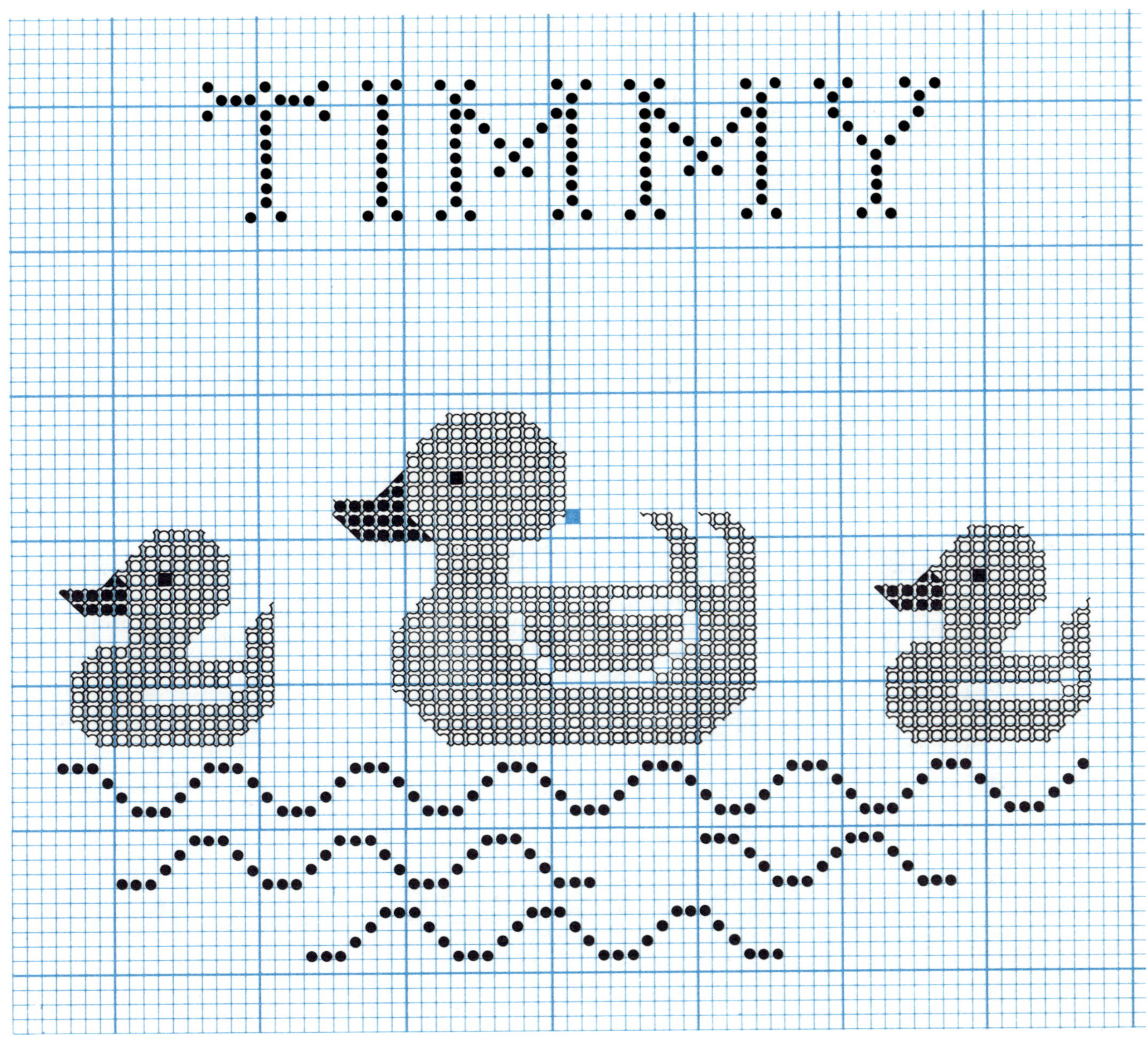

it for whomever you like. Refer to the chart for placement of the letters, adjusting and accommodating for fewer or more letters than I have used for "Timmy." As before, locate the center square of the design before stitching the letters.

5. Remove tape from the edges after the work is finished. Place the cross stitch face down on a padded ironing board and steam press it.

DUCKY BIB	Color key	DMC #
	Gold	742
	Dark Blue	797
	White	
	Black	

Each square equals 1 stitch

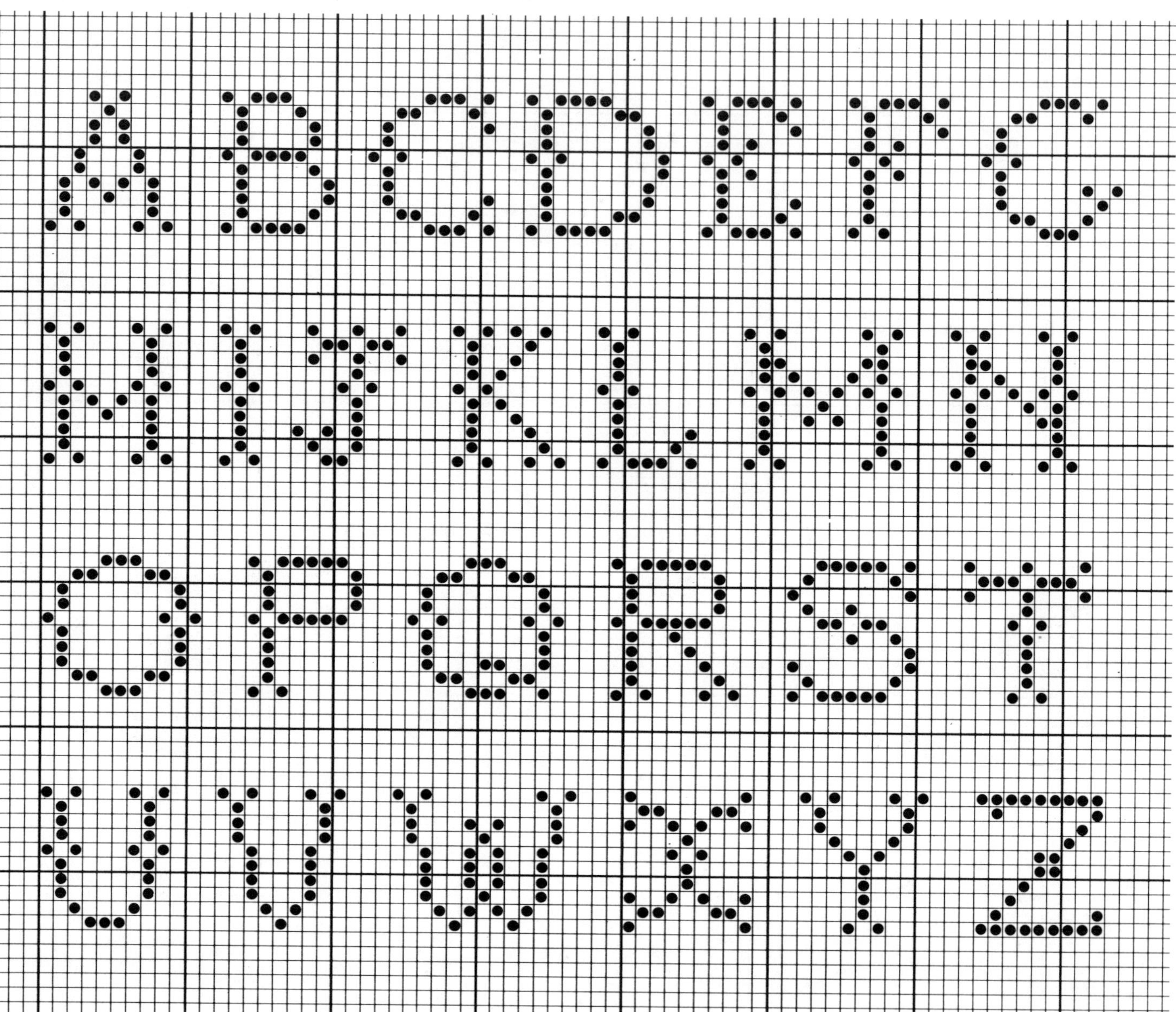

To make bib

1. The pattern piece represents half the bib. Trace the pattern. Fold your cross stitch fabric in half lengthwise and place the tracing on the fold of the fabric.
2. Cut out the bib pattern.
3. If the bib will be backed with vinyl, use the finished bib front as a pattern to cut the shape from the vinyl.
4. With wrong sides facing, bind the top neck area with bias binding. Machine stitch.
5. Leaving approximately 12 inches loose for each tie on either side of the neck, machine stitch binding all around the raw edges of the fabric.
6. If there is no vinyl backing, finish the bib the same way, binding all raw edges.
7. Press all binding and bib from the wrong side.

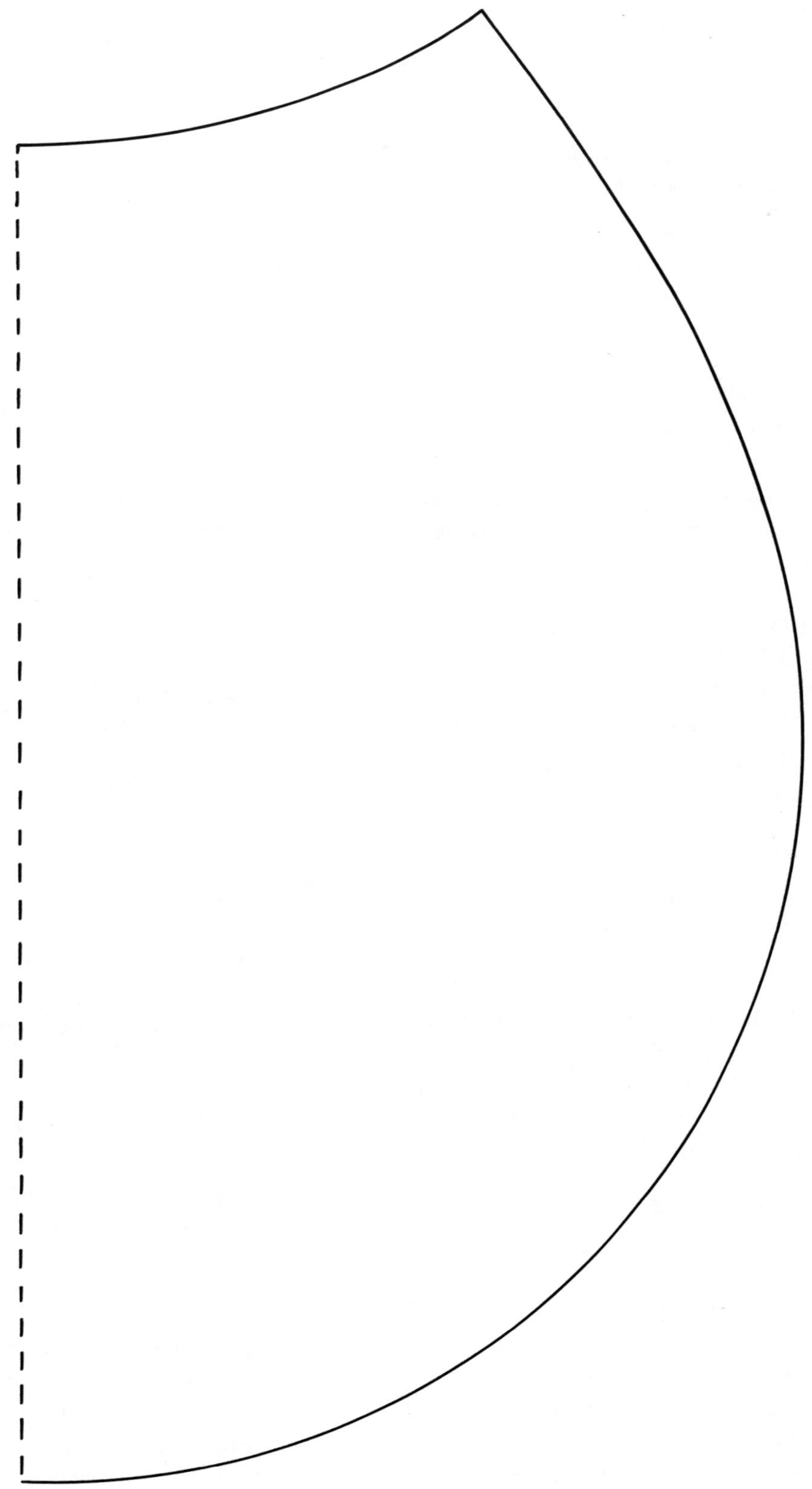

Bib pattern for ducky and bunny bibs

BUNNY BIB

This adorable bib with bunny in the carrot patch would make a wonderful baby gift for a boy or girl. The name is worked with pink floss, but you can change the color if desired for a boy. While premade Aida cloth bibs can be purchased in different sizes, the pattern is provided here should you prefer to make your own. It is easy to cut your own and bind it in the color to match your floss. The floss, binding and bib are completely washable.

Materials

11-count white Aida cloth 9 × 11 inches
embroidery floss in colors indicated on chart
needle
hoop
package of double-fold 1-inch-wide bias binding
9 × 11–inch vinyl for backing (optional)
masking tape (not needed for premade bib)
tracing paper (if pattern is used)

Directions

1. Begin by binding all raw edges with masking tape.
2. Using the charted design provided, find the center square, which is solid.
3. Count the number of squares up and out from that point to the beginning of the first line of the charted design. You will begin with the carrots and bunny. The name will be worked last.
4. Find the center of your fabric by folding it in half vertically, then horizontally.
5. Each square on the graph corresponds to a square on your fabric. Since they are not always the same size, you count but do not measure.
6. Find your starting point for the first stitch. You can begin with the tops of the carrots, or you may want to work on the bunny first, filling in the carrots last. In this way you will be sure that the bunny is perfectly centered and it will be easy to work on the carrots, with even spaces between.

To work the stitches

1. Separate the strands of embroidery floss.
2. Rejoin three strands of floss, approximately 18 inches long, and thread your needle.
3. Follow the chart to determine where each stitch in each color is placed. You can finish the details, such as the red bow, eye, nose, pink inner ear and black outline, last. Notice on the chart that all solid straight lines indicate an outlined area that is worked with a backstitch.
4. Use the letter chart on p. 8 to personalize your design. Refer to the chart for placement of the letters, adjusting and accommodating for fewer or more letters than I have on the "Katey" bib. As before, always begin by finding the center square of the design by counting.
5. Remove tape from the edges after the work is finished. Place the cross stitch

face down on a padded ironing board and steam press.

To make bib

1. Use the pattern on p. 9. The pattern piece represents half the bib. Trace the pattern. Fold fabric in half lengthwise and place pattern on fold.
2. Cut out bib pattern.
3. If the bib will be backed with vinyl, use the finished bib front as a pattern to cut the shape from the vinyl.
4. With wrong sides facing, bind the top neck area with bias binding. Machine stitch.
5. Leaving approximately 12 inches loose for tying, machine stitch binding all around the raw edges of the fabric, leaving another 12 inches at the end for the second tie.
6. If there is no vinyl backing, finish the bib the same way, binding all raw edges.
7. Press all binding and bib from the wrong side.

BUNNY BIB	Color key	DMC #
	Pink	3326
	Orange	740
	Red	666
	Green	702
	Light Pink	818
	Light Brown	436
	Black	
	Outline—Black	

Each square equals 1 stitch

DO-RE-ME PLAQUE

This delightful little girl can sing the scales and will add a cheerful note to any child's room. It's a quick and easy design to stitch, and you can finish it with a frame from the five-and-ten. If you want to add a matte, choose a color to match the floss, perhaps the blue from the notes or the yellow from her hair ribbons. The frame might also be one of the colors from the design. Any way you choose to finish it, this 5 × 7–inch picture is sure to please.

Materials

11-count white Aida cloth, 8 × 10 inches
embroidery floss in colors indicated on chart
needle
hoop
5 × 7–inch frame
masking tape

Directions

1. Begin by binding all raw edges of the Aida cloth with masking tape.
2. Using the charted design provided, find the center square, which is solid.
3. Count the number of squares up and out from that point to the beginning of the first line of the charted design.
4. Find the center of your fabric by folding it in half vertically, then horizontally.
5. Each square on the graph corresponds to a square on your fabric. Since they are not always the same size, you count but do not measure.
6. Find the starting point for the first stitch. This will be the little girl's black hair.

To work the stitches

1. Separate the strands of embroidery floss.
2. Rejoin three strands of floss, approximately 18 inches long, and thread your needle.
3. Follow the chart to determine where each stitch in each color is placed. Some stitchers prefer to finish all stitches in one color before changing to another color. Others like to finish a section of the design, changing colors as needed. For this design, either method is fine.
4. All straight, solid lines on the chart indicate a black outline stitch such as on the little girl's shoes for straps.
5. When you have finished the cross stitch, remove the tape from all edges.
6. Place the cross stitch face down on a padded ironing board and steam press.

To finish

1. Trim the excess Aida cloth around the design so it measures 6½ × 9 inches.
2. With the cross stitch face down, center the backing from the frame on the back of the work.
3. Pull the fabric to the back and tape it tautly with the masking tape. (See p. xiii for framing directions.)
4. Check the front of the design as you do this to be sure you aren't distorting the picture.
5. Place finished work in the frame and hang.

DO-RE-ME PLAQUE

Color key	DMC #
Blue	799
Pink	894
Red	892
Flesh	754
Yellow	444
Black	

Each square equals 1 stitch

CHICKY TOWEL EDGING

Add a little pizzazz to a set of towels for a toddler. He or she will love having a personalized towel with little chickens marching across the edge. Since the floss and Aida cloth are cotton, it can be washed with no problem. Since the cross stitching is very quick and easy to do, this makes a good bazaar item as well as a quick last-minute gift to make.

Materials

11-count white Aida cloth 4–5 inches wide and as long as the towel's width
embroidery floss in colors indicated on chart
needle
hoop
package of red rickrack
masking tape

Directions

1. Begin by binding all raw edges of the Aida cloth with masking tape.
2. Using the charted design provided, find the center square, which is solid.
3. Count the number of squares up and out from that point to the beginning of the first line of the charted design.
4. Find the center of your fabric by folding it in half vertically, then horizontally.
5. Each square on the graph corresponds to a square on your fabric. Since they are not always the same size, you count but do not measure. Don't make the mistake of measuring the space between each chick for placement. Always count the squares on the chart and the squares on the fabric.

To work the stitches

1. Separate the strands of embroidery floss.
2. Rejoin three strands of floss, approximately 18 inches long, and thread your needle.
3. Follow the chart to determine where each stitch in each color is placed. In this case the chicks are all one color. You simply keep repeating the design all the way across your Aida strip.
4. Fill in the black stitch for each eye and use a backstitch of black floss for the legs. The solid lines on the chart indicate where to place the outline stitches.

To finish

1. Pin a row of rickrack along the fifth line of squares on the fabric above the tallest chick.
2. Repeat under the chicken's feet. Machine stitch.
3. Remove the tape from the raw edges and place the cross stitch face down on a padded ironing board. Steam press.
4. Trim the width of the strip so it is approximately 3½ inches wide.
5. Turn the raw edges under so there are about three rows of Aida squares on top and bottom of rickrack. Press. Turn side edges under and press.
6. Place this in position about 2 inches from the bottom edge of the towel and machine stitch together along all edges.

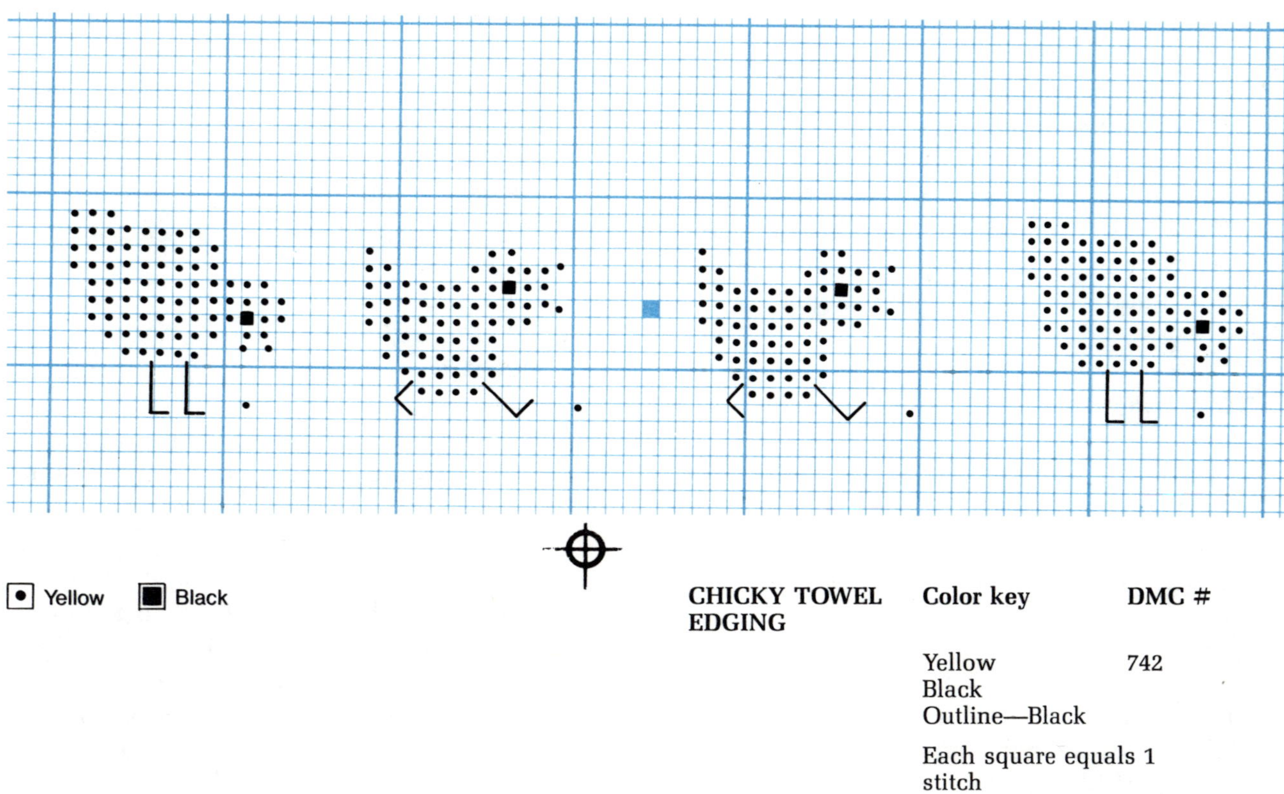

CHICKY TOWEL EDGING

Color key	DMC #
Yellow	742
Black	
Outline—Black	

Each square equals 1 stitch

ABC BABY PILLOW

Choose a gingham fabric in the color of your choice. This pillow was designed by Robby Smith and she used a pink gingham in tiny checks. The finished size is 10 × 10 inches and the cross stitched area is 5 × 5 inches. This is a sweet addition to the carriage or crib and makes a lovely newborn gift.

Materials

1/3 yard pink gingham fabric
14-count white Aida, 6 × 6 inches
embroidery floss in colors indicated on chart
needle
hoop
1 1/2 yards of 1-inch-wide eyelet (there will be extra)
25 inches of 1/2-inch-wide white eyelet
package of blue piping
20 inches of 1/4-inch-wide satin ribbon
polyester stuffing
masking tape

Directions

1. Begin by binding all raw edges of the Aida cloth with masking tape.
2. Using the charted design provided, find the center square, which is solid.
3. Count the number of squares up and out from that point to the beginning of the first line of the charted design.
4. Find the center of the fabric by folding it in half vertically, then horizontally.
5. Each square on the graph corresponds to a square on your fabric. Since they are not always the same size, you count but do not measure.
6. Find your starting point for the first stitch.

To work the stitches

1. Separate the strands of embroidery floss.
2. Rejoin two strands of floss, approximately 18 inches long, and thread your needle.
3. With the Aida secured in the embroidery hoop, begin stitching the blocks.
4. Continue to fill in the stitches for each area according to the chart.
5. Next stitch the border design, checking your work often to be sure your corners will meet and that you haven't miscounted.
6. When finished, remove the tape from the edges and place the work face down on a padded ironing board. Steam press.

To assemble pillow top

1. Cut two pieces of pink gingham 10 1/2 × 10 1/2 inches.
2. With right sides facing and raw edges aligned, pin the 1-inch-wide eyelet around the edges of one piece of fabric. Machine stitch.
3. With right sides facing and raw edges aligned, stitch the piping around the Aida cloth, overlapping ends at one corner.
4. Next, with right sides facing and raw

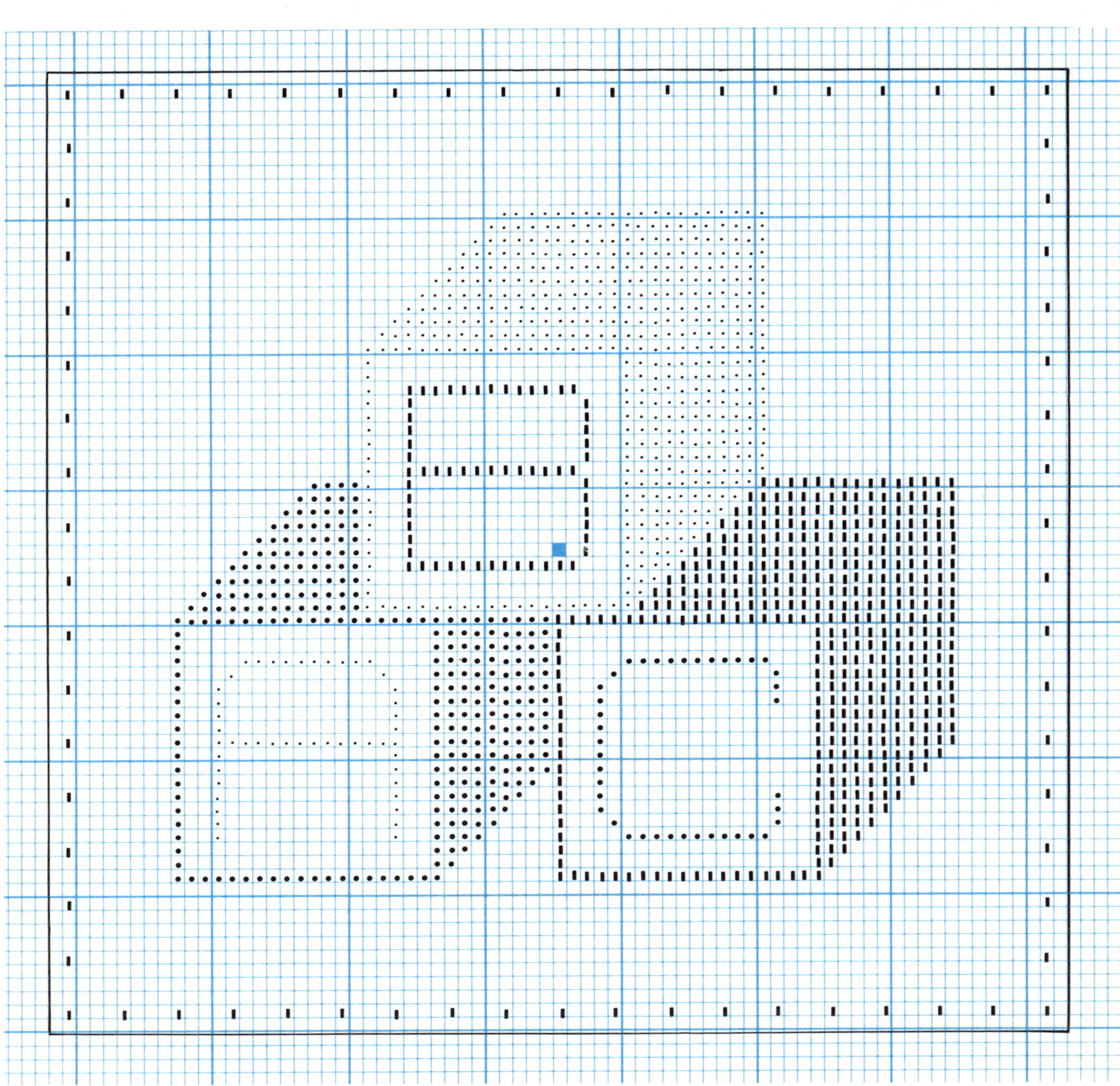

ABC BABY PILLOW

Color key	**DMC #**
Blue	3325
Pink	776
Yellow	445

Each square equals 1 stitch

edges aligned, pin the 1/2-inch eyelet around all edges of the Aida cloth.

5. From the wrong side, stitch the eyelet to the Aida, using the piping stitches as a guide.
6. Cut the satin ribbon into four equal parts and make four bows. Tack each one to a corner of the cross stitch Aida square.
7. Center the cross stitch on the gingham pillow top and machine stitch at the edge of the Aida fabric close to the piping (a zipper foot on your machine is helpful for this).

To finish pillow

1. Flatten the outside ruffle and pin the corners to the pillow top to hold temporarily out of the way.
2. Pin the second gingham piece face down over pillow, with the ruffle between. Machine stitch all around three sides and four corners.
3. Turn the pillow right side out and press from the wrong side.
4. Fill with stuffing and slipstitch the opening closed.

MARY HAD A LITTLE LAMB

Use soft pastel colors to create a darling plaque for a child's room. The background is white Aida, which means that the bottom portion and the lamb do not have to be filled with stitches. The green and yellow background takes a bit of patience, but the results are well worth the time spent. The matte board and frame match the colors perfectly and they are simply standard five-and-ten products. The finished plaque when framed is 8½ × 10½ inches. The cross stitch area is 5 × 7 inches and will fit a standard frame as is.

Materials

14-count white Aida cloth, 8 × 10 inches
embroidery floss in colors indicated on chart
needle
hoop
matte and frame
masking tape

Directions

1. Begin by binding all raw edges of the Aida cloth with masking tape.
2. Using the charted design provided, find the center square, which is solid.
3. Count the number of squares up and out from that point to the beginning of the first line of the charted design.
4. Find the center of your fabric by folding it in half vertically, then horizontally.
5. Each square on the graph corresponds to a square on your fabric. Since they are not always the same size, you count but do not measure.
6. Find the starting point for the first stitch. This will be green and you will continue for the number of squares across and down to fill in the background, leaving the squares that will later be filled with yellow floss unworked.

To work the stitches

1. Separate the strands of embroidery floss.
2. Rejoin two strands of floss, approximately 18 inches long, and thread your needle.
3. Follow the chart to determine where each stitch in each color is placed. After filling in the required number of squares on the background, add the pink and then blue details on the white lamb.
4. Find the starting stitch for the letters the same way as before, and be sure all your letters are appropriately spaced according to the chart.
5. When you have finished the cross stitch, remove the tape from all edges.
6. Place the cross stitch face down on a padded ironing board and steam press.

To finish

1. Trim the excess Aida cloth around the design so it measures 6½ × 8½ inches.
2. With the cross stitch face down, center

● Light Green ⬤ Light Blue ■ Pink ✲ Yellow

the backing from the frame on the back of the work.

3. Pull the fabric to the back and tape it tautly with the masking tape. (See p. xiii for framing directions.)
4. Check the front of the design as you do this to be sure you aren't distorting the picture.
5. Place the finished work in the frame and hang.

MARY HAD A LITTLE LAMB

Color key	DMC #
Light Green	955
Light Blue	827
Pink	776
Yellow	445

Each square equals 1 stitch

CHOO-CHOO BIRTH ANNOUNCEMENT

When that new baby boy arrives, make this cross stitch birth announcement complete with his name, birth date and weight. It will be a welcome gift for the new parents and can be hung in the baby's room as a permanent decoration. This easy and quick-to-stitch project is 8½ × 11 inches when framed. The cross stitch area is 5 × 7 inches.

Materials

14-count white Aida cloth, 8 × 10 inches
embroidery floss in colors indicated on chart
needle
hoop
matte and frame
masking tape

Directions

1. Begin by binding all raw edges of the Aida cloth with masking tape.
2. Using the charted design provided, find the center square, which is solid.
3. Count the number of squares up and out from that point to the beginning of the first line of the charted design.
4. Find the center of your fabric by folding it in half vertically, then horizontally.
5. Each square on the graph corresponds to a square on your fabric. Since they are not always the same size, you count but do not measure.
6. Find the starting point for the first stitch. You might want to work the trains first, later filling in the clouds and outlining the words.

To work the stitches

1. Separate the strands of embroidery floss.
2. Rejoin two strands of floss, approximately 18 inches long, and thread your needle.
3. Follow the chart to determine where each stitch in each color is placed.
4. The straight, solid lines on the chart indicate the black outline stitches. These are backstitches used for the letters.
5. When you have finished the cross stitch, remove the tape from all edges.
6. Place the cross stitch face down on a padded ironing board and steam press.

To finish

1. Trim the excess Aida cloth around the design so it measures 6½ × 8½ inches.
2. With the cross stitch face down, center the backing from the frame on the back of the work.
3. Pull the fabric to the back and tape it tautly with the masking tape. (See p. xiii for framing directions.)
4. Check the front of the design as you do this to be sure you aren't distorting the picture.
5. Place the finished work in the frame and hang.

● Light Blue ⊡ Yellow ✱ Black ◈ Pink △ Lavendar

CHOO-CHOO BIRTH ANNOUNCEMENT

Color key	DMC #
Light Blue	827
Yellow	445
Pink	894
Lavender	210
Black	

Letters and numbers—Black

Each square equals 1 stitch

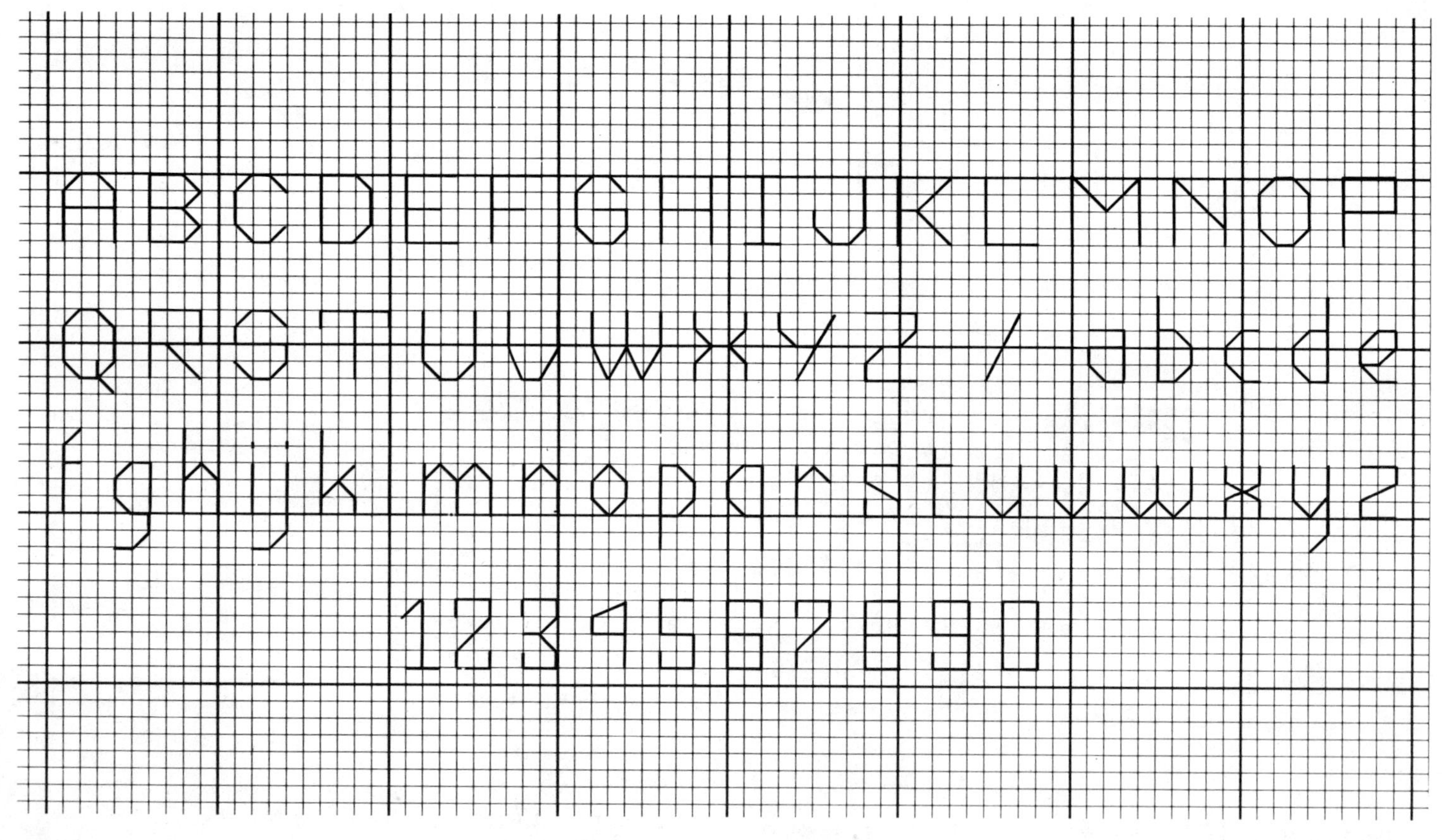
ABCDEFGHIJKLMNOP
QRSTUVWXYZ / abcde
fghijk mnopqrstuvwxyz
1234567890

MINIATURE HANG-UPS

These miniature pictures are perfect for a small area in a baby's room. They are terrific shower gifts or bazaar items because they take very little time to make. They are also inexpensive to frame. The pop-together frames come in various sizes and colors and are sold in craft stores and the five-and-ten. You do the embroidery right in the frame, then cut away the excess fabric all around when you're finished. These frames are 2½ inches in diameter.

Materials

TEDDY BEAR: 14-count yellow Aida cloth, 4 × 4 inches
SAILBOAT: 14-count blue Aida cloth, 4 × 4 inches
ALPHABETS: 14-count white Aida cloth, 4 × 4 inches
embroidery floss in colors indicated on charts
needle
2½-inch frames in colors to match each design

Directions

1. Using the charted designs provided, begin by finding the center square for each project, which is solid.
2. Count the number of squares up and out from that point to the beginning of the first line of the charted design.
3. Secure the Aida cloth in the frame and count the squares to find the center square of the fabric.
4. Each square on the graph corresponds to a square on your fabric. Since they are not always the same size, you count but do not measure.
5. Find the starting point for the first stitch.

To work the stitches

1. Separate the strands of embroidery floss.
2. Rejoin two strands for all colors except white, of which you will use three strands. Because the sailboat background is blue, the white will be brighter when three strands are used. Cut a length of floss approximately 18 inches long and thread your needle.
3. Follow the charts to determine where each stitch in each color is placed.
4. When you have finished the cross stitch, cut away the excess fabric as close to the frame as possible and hang the miniature picture.

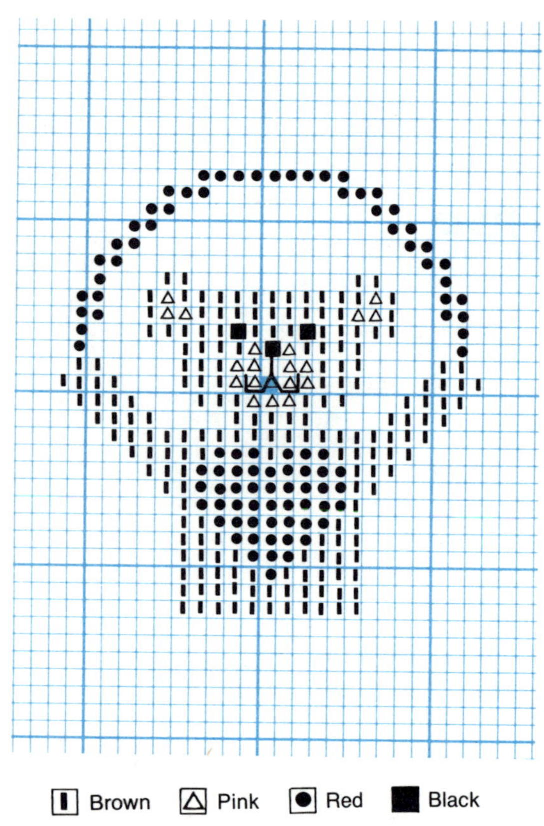

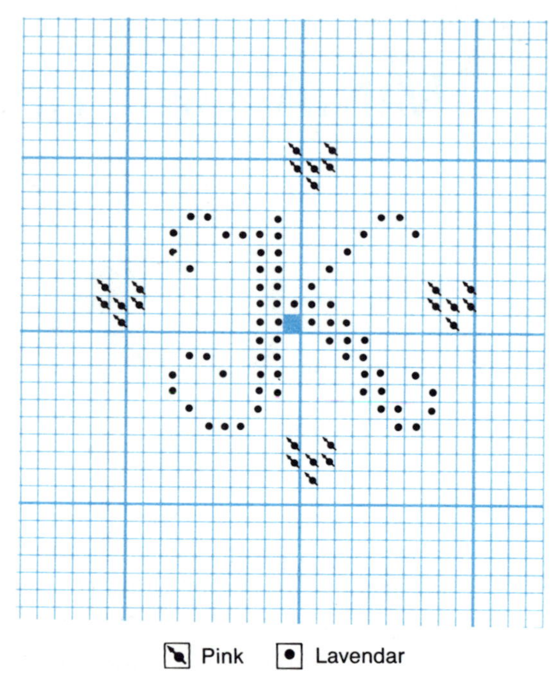

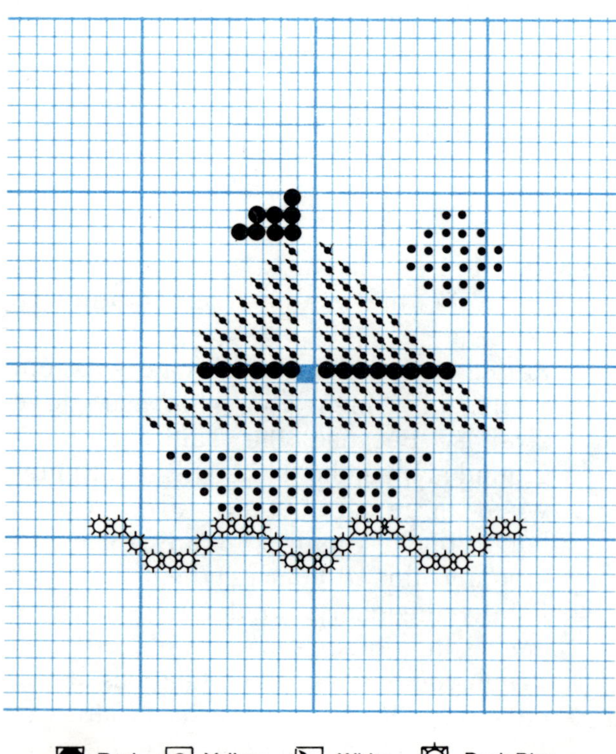

MINIATURE HANG-UPS

Color key	DMC #
Teddy Bear	
Red	999
Brown	632
Pink	894
Black	
Sailboat	
Red	999
Yellow	742
White	
Dark Blue	797
Alphabet—B—	
Pink	894
Green	955

Note: Pick up B from alphabet

Alphabet—K—	
Pink	894
Lavender	208

Each square equals 1 stitch

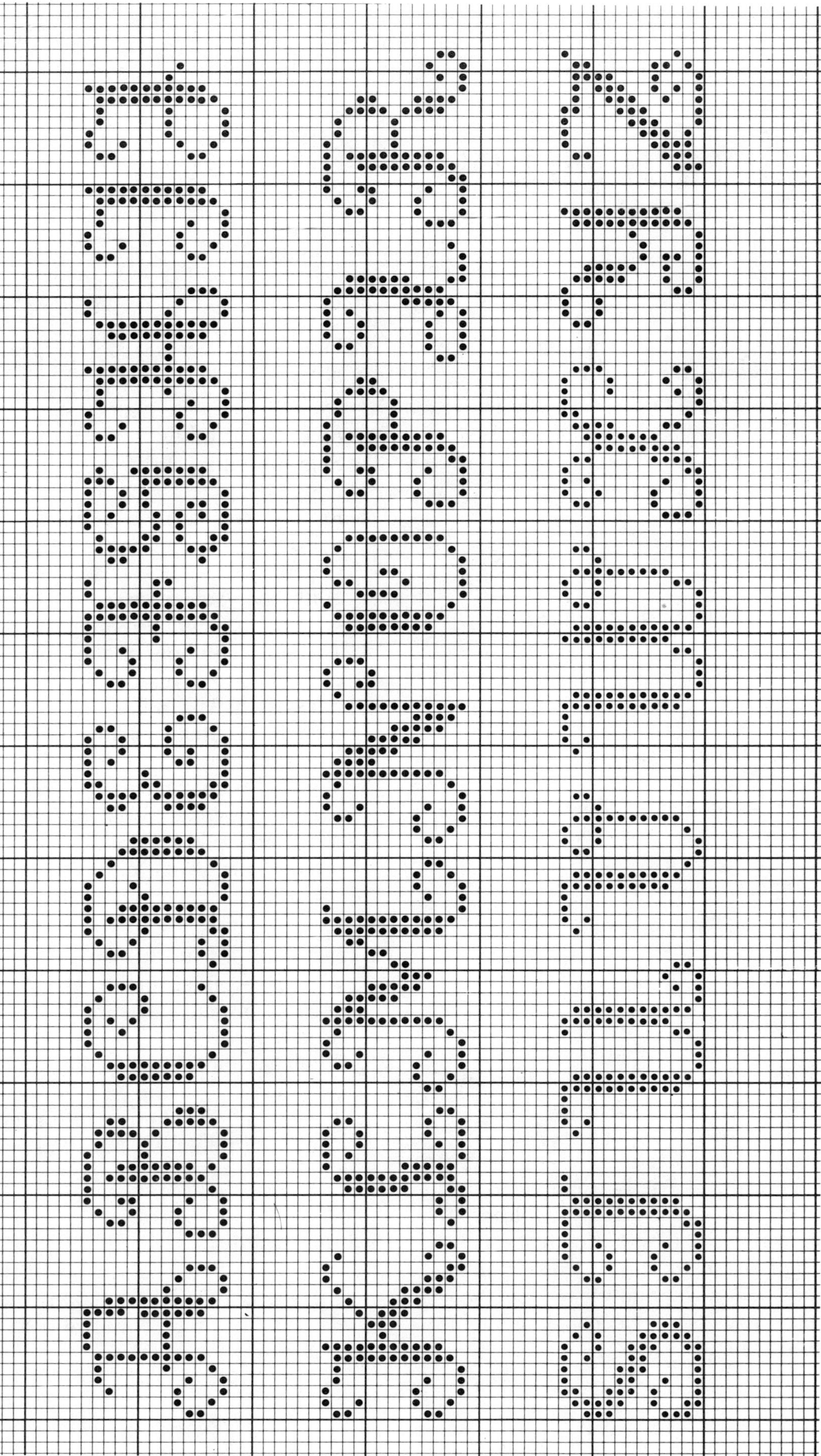

SHHHH PILLOW

A little 6-inch-square pillow edged in crochet lace tells everyone when baby is sleeping. Hang it on the doorknob for all to see. If you'd like, it can be framed as a little room decoration as well. It's the perfect shower gift.

Materials

14-count pink Aida cloth, 8 × 8 inches
embroidery floss in colors indicated on chart
needle
hoop
25 inches of lace or eyelet
25 inches of blue piping
12 inches of 1/2-inch satin ribbon
backing fabric, 6 1/2 × 6 1/2 inches
polyester stuffing
masking tape

Directions

1. Begin by binding all raw edges of the Aida cloth with masking tape.
2. Using the charted design provided, find the center square, which is solid.
3. Count the number of squares up and out from that point to the beginning of the first line of the charted design.
4. Find the center of the fabric by folding it in half vertically, then horizontally.
5. Each square on the graph corresponds to a square on your fabric. Since they are not always the same size, you count but do not measure.
6. Find your starting point for the first stitch.

To work the stitches

1. Separate the strands of embroidery floss.
2. Rejoin two strands of floss, approximately 18 inches long, and thread your needle.
3. With the Aida secured in the embroidery hoop, begin stitching the design.
4. The solid outline of the baby's hands and face are done in black floss, using a backstitch. The ruffles of the pillow are blue backstitches. Place them as indicated on the chart.
5. When you are finished, remove the tape from all edges and place the work face down on a padded ironing board. Steam press. Trim Aida cloth to 6 1/2 inches square.

To assemble pillow top

1. With right sides facing and raw edges aligned, stitch the piping around the Aida cloth.
2. Stitch the lace trim around the edge the same way.
3. Pin the ends of the ribbon to the pillow front approximately 1 inch in from each edge.

To finish pillow

1. With right sides facing and raw edges aligned, pin the backing fabric to the pillow top. The ruffles and ribbon loop are between.

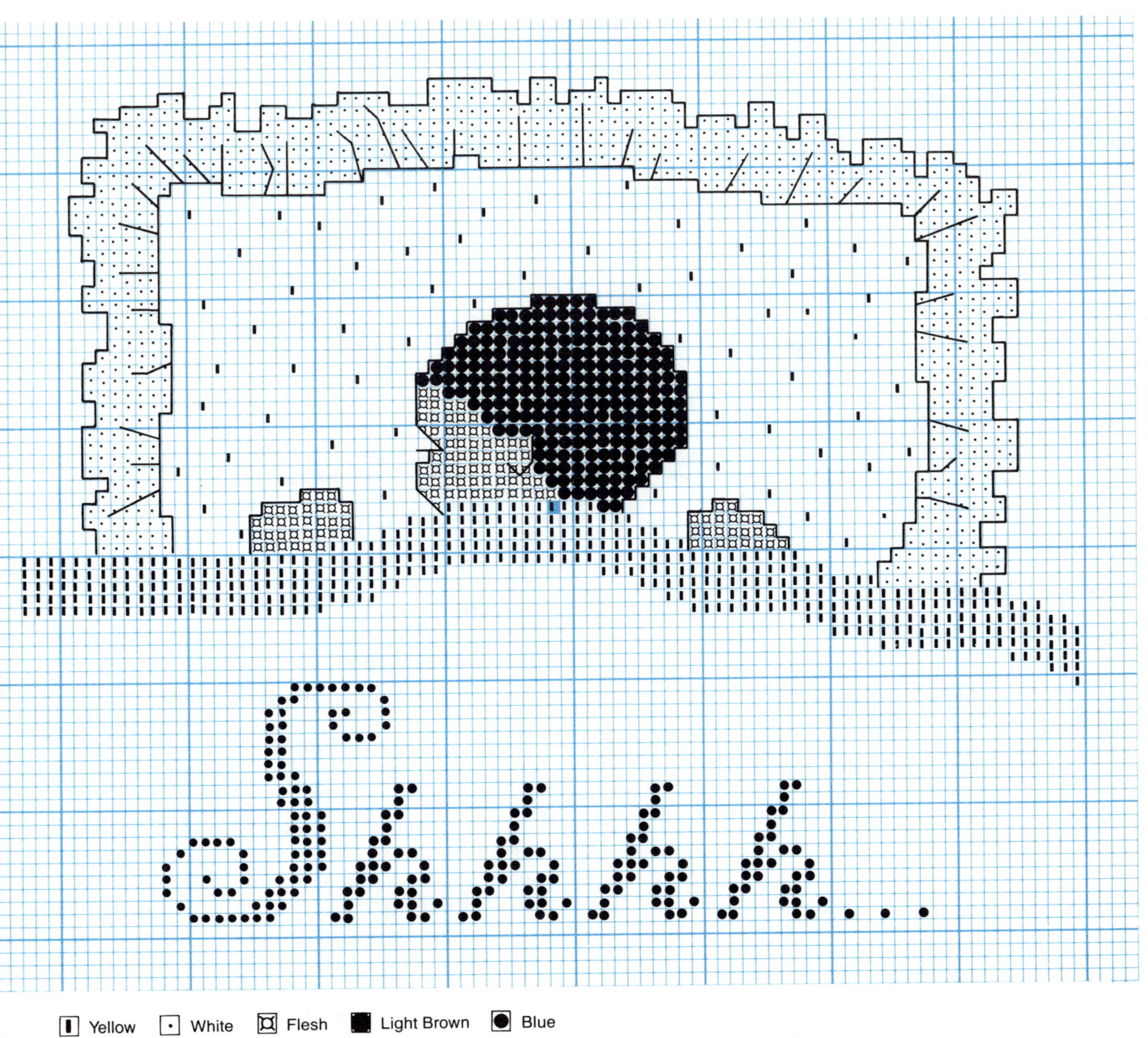

2. From the wrong side, machine stitch the backing to the pillow around three sides and four corners, leaving an opening for turning.
3. Turn the pillow right side out and press from the wrong side.
4. Stuff the pillow and slipstitch the opening closed.

SHHHH PILLOW

Color key	**DMC #**
Yellow	726
White	
Flesh	954
Light Brown	402
Blue	799

Outline on pillow ruffle—Blue
Outline on hands, face and car —Black

Each square equals 1 stitch

"BABY SLEEPING" DOOR HANGER

When baby is sleeping and you want quiet time, hang this little reminder over the doorknob. It's a sweet gift to make for the mother-to-be or to give at a baby shower. I've used pink floss on a navy blue Aida cloth background, surrounded by a white eyelet and pink dotted Swiss ruffle. You can choose another color, such as yellow or pale green, if you don't yet know the sex of the child. The finished pillow is 6 × 9 inches including the ruffles.

Materials

14-count navy blue Aida cloth, 6 × 9 inches
embroidery floss in colors indicated on chart
needle
hoop
22 inches of pregathered 1/2-inch-wide eyelet
strip of pink dotted Swiss, 1 × 45 inches (can be pieced)
fabric for backing, 4 1/2 × 7 inches
12 inches of 1/2-inch-wide satin ribbon
polyester stuffing
masking tape

Directions

1. Begin by binding all raw edges of the Aida cloth with masking tape.
2. Using the charted design provided, find the center square, which is solid.
3. Count the number of squares up and out from that point to the beginning of the first line of the charted design.
4. Find the center of the fabric by folding it in half vertically, then horizontally.
5. Each square on the graph corresponds to a square on your fabric. Since they are not always the same size, you count but do not measure.
6. Find your starting point for the first stitch.

To work the stitches

1. Separate the strands of embroidery floss.
2. Rejoin two strands of floss, approximately 18 inches long, and thread your needle.
3. With the Aida secured in the embroidery hoop, begin stitching the letters. Check your work often to be sure your letters are evenly spaced and that the word "Baby" is centered above "Sleeping."
4. You can follow the chart to fill in the stars, or place them at random on the background.
5. When finished, remove the tape from all edges and place the work face down on a padded ironing board. Steam press.

To assemble pillow top

1. With right sides facing and raw edges aligned, machine stitch the eyelet around the edge of the Aida cloth.
2. With right sides facing and raw edges aligned, stitch the short ends of the dotted Swiss strip together.

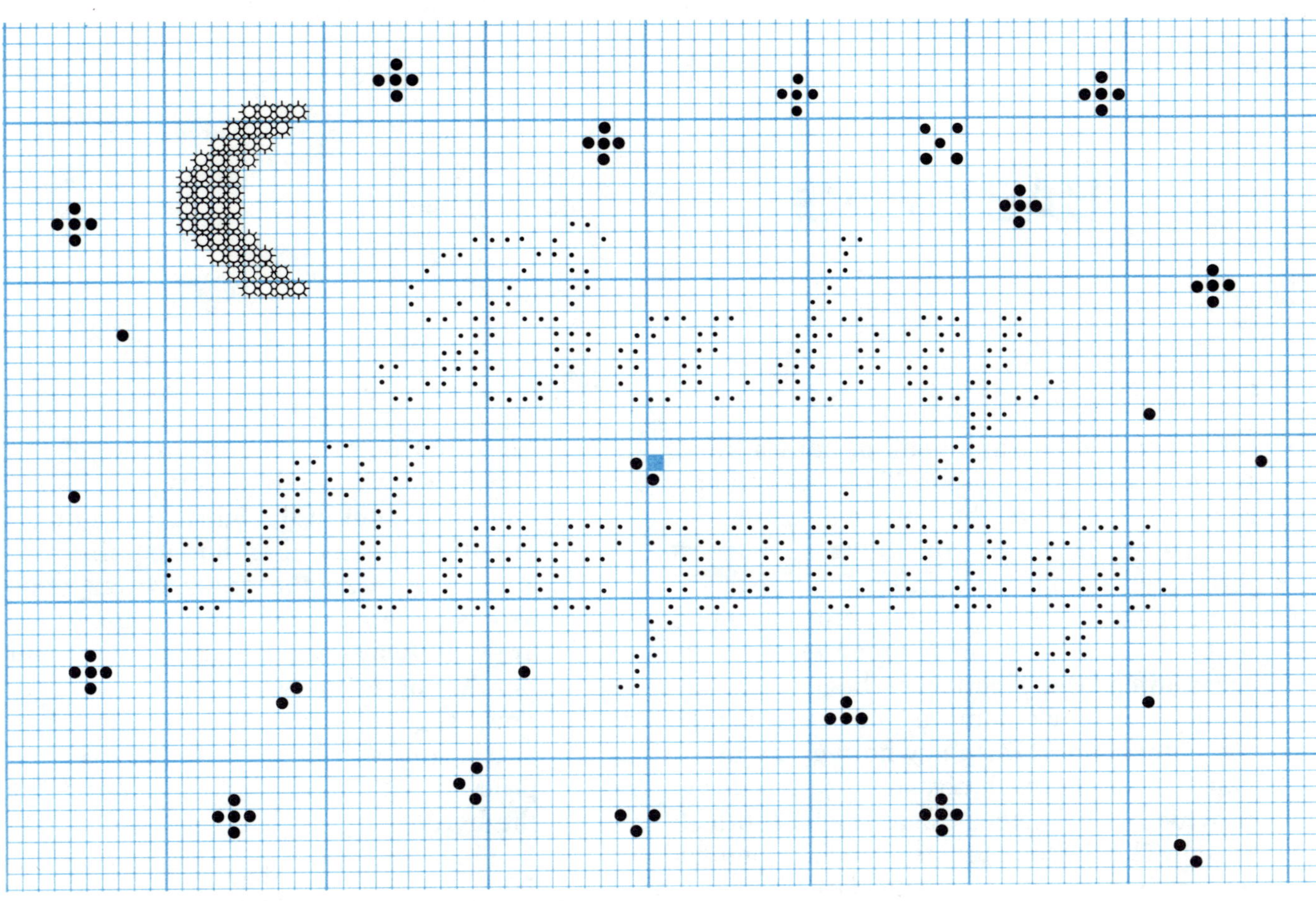

"BABY SLEEPING" DOOR HANGER

Color key	DMC #
Pink	3326
Yellow	743
White	

Each square equals 1 stitch

3. Turn one raw edge under 1/4 inch and press.
4. Turn under another 1/4 inch, press and stitch.
5. Divide the fabric into four equal parts and mark with a pin.
6. With right sides facing and raw edges aligned, gather the fabric as you pin it between these points from corner to corner around the pillow.
7. Divide the satin ribbon in half lengthwise and pin each end approximately 1 1/2 inches in from each outer corner on the top for hanging. The loop will be toward the center of the pillow top. Pin in place temporarily to keep it out of the stitching area.
8. Machine stitch all around, leaving a 1/4-inch seam allowance.

To finish pillow

1. With right sides facing and raw edges aligned, pin the backing fabric to the pillow top. The ruffles and ribbon loop are between.
2. From the wrong side, machine stitch the backing to the pillow, using the ruffle stitches as a guide. Stitch around three sides and four corners.
3. Trim the corners and turn the pillow right side out. Press from the back side.
4. Stuff the pillow and slipstitch the opening closed.

BABY BAG

Make a duffel bag to tote all of baby's things when you go on an outing. This one is amply roomy for diapers, bottle, toys, change of clothes and some of your things. There are three pockets on the front for the things you need most, and the drawstring opening makes it easy to rummage around inside. The cross stitch "Baby" label can be personalized with your baby's name if you make it after the baby is born. For a newborn gift, you can start before the birth day and use the design provided here. Choose colors and fabric to match. The finished tote is 15 inches high and 32 inches around when fully opened.

Materials

11-count white Aida cloth, 5 × 9 inches
embroidery floss in colors indicated on chart
needle
hoop
solid fabric, 16 × 33 inches
solid fabric circle, 10½ inches in diameter
printed fabric, 6 × 15 inches
3 yards cording
masking tape

Directions

1. Begin by binding all raw edges of the Aida cloth with masking tape.
2. Using the charted design provided, find the center square, which is solid.
3. Count the number of squares up and out from that point to the beginning of the first line of the charted design.
4. Find the center of the fabric by folding it in half vertically, then horizontally.
5. Each square on the graph corresponds to a square on your fabric. Since they are not always the same size, you count but do not measure.
6. Find your starting point for the first stitch. You will begin with the "B" and proceed with all the letters before doing the border.

To work the stitches

1. Separate the strands of embroidery floss.
2. Rejoin three strands of floss, approximately 18 inches long, and thread your needle.
3. With the Aida cloth secured in the hoop, begin stitching the letters.
4. When working on the border, check your work often to be sure your corners will meet and that you haven't miscounted.
5. When finished, remove the tape and place the work face down on a padded ironing board. Steam press.

To make bag

1. Turn one long edge of the solid fabric piece under ¼ inch and press.
2. Fold this edge down to the wrong side 1½ inches and hem.
3. Machine stitch ½ inch from top edge to

Pink Green

BABY BAG

Color key	DMC #
Pink	893
Green	913

Each square equals 1 stitch

create a channel between the first and second stitch lines for the cording.

4. Cut printed fabric piece to 5 × 14½ inches.
5. Turn one long edge under ¼ inch and press. Turn under another ¼ inch, press and stitch. Repeat at side edges.
6. Center and pin the printed fabric on the solid fabric piece with the bottom, raw edges even.
7. Divide the printed fabric into thirds and draw a light pencil line on the fabric at these points.
8. Stitch along side edges and down each marked line to create pockets. Backstitch to reinforce corners of each pocket.
9. Cut two pieces of the print fabric 1½ × 7 inches. Cut two pieces 1½ × 5 inches.
10. Trim Aida cloth so the finished cross stitch piece is 3¼ × 7 inches.
11. With right sides facing and raw edges aligned, stitch the border pieces to the Aida cloth with a ¼-inch seam allowance. Open seams and press.
12. Turn raw edges under ¼ inch all around and press.
13. Pin "Baby" 1½ inches above the pockets, so it is centered on the bag.

To finish bag

1. With right sides facing and raw edges aligned, machine stitch the short ends of the solid fabric together, using a ¼-inch seam allowance.
2. With right sides facing, pin the fabric circle around the bottom raw edge of the bag with the raw edge of the pockets between.
3. Machine stitch around. Turn right side out.
4. Cut a slit on either side of the channel through top layer of fabric only.
5. Whipstitch around the raw edges of the slit for cording opening.
6. Weave the cording through one slit all the way around and out the same slit.
7. Repeat on the reverse side. Tie the ends together in a knot and pull drawstrings to close the bag top.

BIRTH ANNOUNCEMENT SAMPLER

There is nothing nicer for a new baby's parents than a handmade gift. And one that is personalized with baby's name, birth date and weight is something to treasure forever. The designs surrounding the announcement are done in soft pastels and the letters can be worked in the color of your choice. In this case, the "Jessica Lynn" is a pretty, soft pink shade. The finished project measures $9\frac{1}{2} \times 12$ inches without the 2-inch-wide matte board.

Materials

14-count white Aida cloth, 12 × 15 inches
embroidery floss in colors indicated on chart
needle
hoop
frame with matte board
masking tape

Directions

1. Begin by binding all raw edges of the Aida cloth with masking tape.
2. Using the charted design provided, find the center square, which is solid.
3. Count the number of squares up and out from that point to the beginning of the first line of the charted design. For this project it is best to work the borders first so that you can center and accurately place each design element.
4. Find the center of your fabric by folding it in half vertically, then horizontally.
5. Each square on the graph corresponds to a square on your fabric. Since they are not always the same size, you count but do not measure.
6. Find the starting point for the first stitch.

To work the stitches

1. Separate the strands of embroidery floss.
2. Rejoin two strands of blue floss, approximately 18 inches long, and thread the needle to start the border.
3. Follow the chart to determine where each stitch is placed. When working a border, stop to check the number of stitches you have worked so that all corners meet as indicated on the chart. In this way you avoid having to pull out extra stitches.
4. Complete all the lines around each design before filling in the design. In this way you will have little boxes in which to work the individual designs.
5. Center and space the numbers and letters in the middle square outlined by a border. Check your work as you go along to be sure each letter and number is evenly spaced.

To finish

1. Remove the masking tape and place the finished work face down on a padded ironing board. Steam press.

Blue
Light Blue
Pink
Lavendar
Yellow
Green

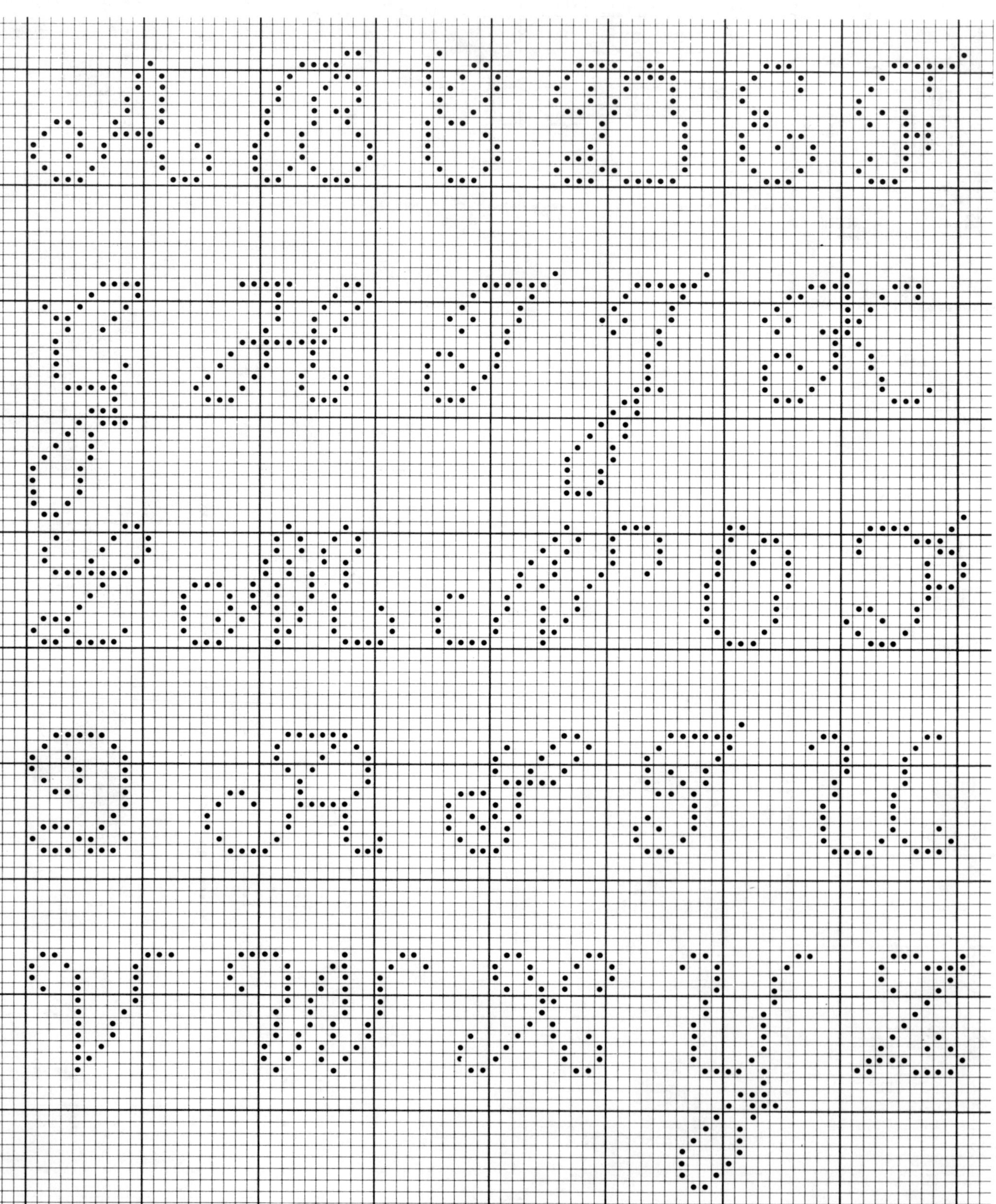

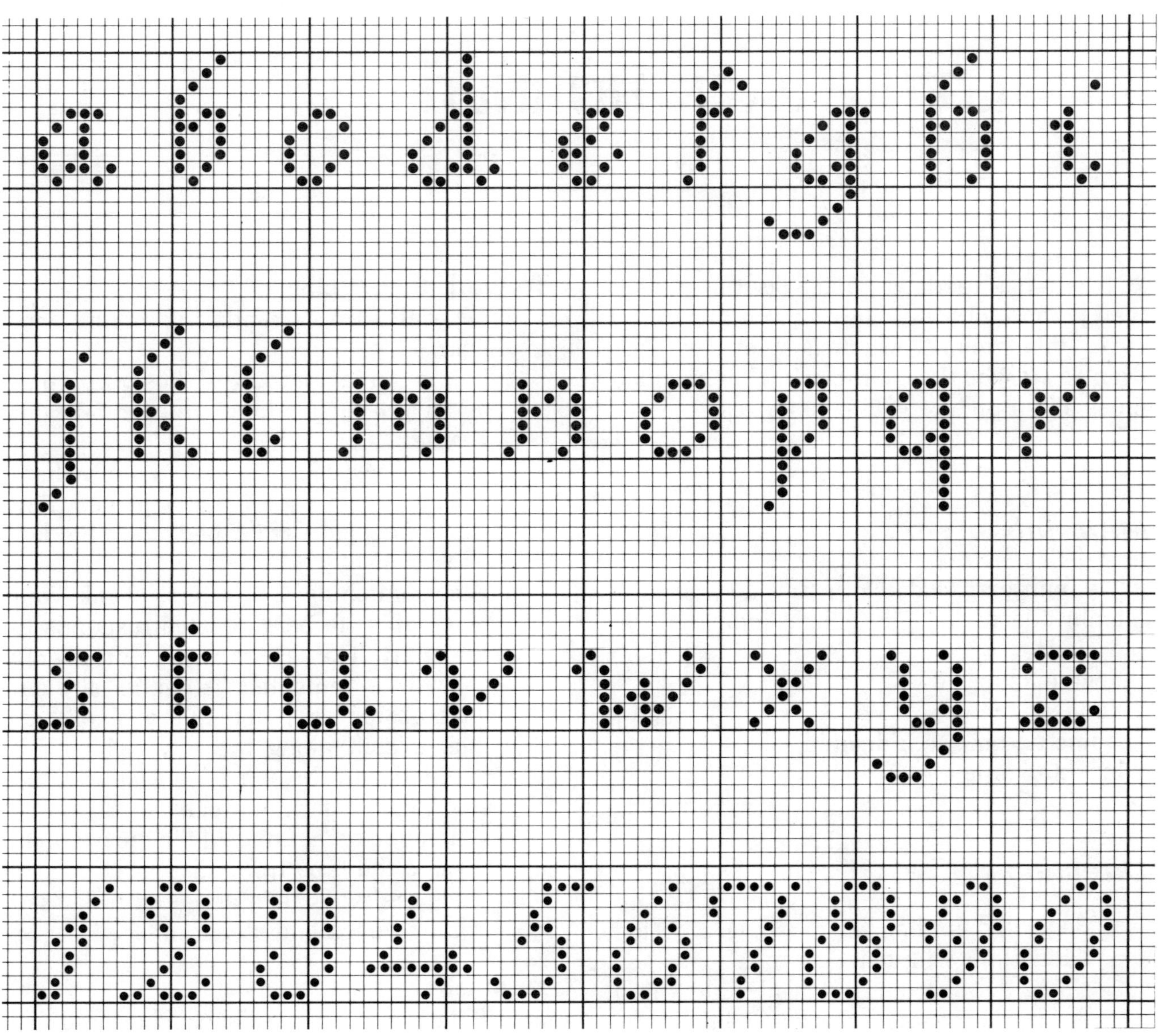

2. Place the work face down on the backing board of the frame and tape to the back. (See p. xiii for framing details.)
3. Check the front of your work as you do this to be sure the picture and border are not distorted. It takes extra care to align the borders so they aren't crooked.
4. Place the matte board over the front of the work and set into the frame for hanging.

BIRTH ANNOUNCEMENT SAMPLER

Color key	DMC #
Blue	826
Light Blue	827
Pink	605
Lavender	210
Yellow	307
Green	955

Each square equals 1 stitch

LITTLE JACK HORNER

"Oh what a good boy am I" is the perfect wall plaque for a little boy's room. It's fun to make this project, which is a classic children's storybook character. The finished cross stitch picture is 8 × 10 inches.

Materials

11-count ecru Aida cloth 10 × 12 inches
embroidery floss in colors indicated on chart
needle
hoop
frame and matte if desired
masking tape

Directions

1. Begin by binding all raw edges of the Aida cloth with masking tape.
2. Using the charted design provided, find the center square, which is solid.
3. Count the number of squares up and out from that point to the beginning of the first line of the charted design.
4. Find the center of your fabric by folding it in half vertically and then horizontally.
5. Each square on the graph corresponds to a square on your fabric. Since they are not always the same size, you count but do not measure.
6. Find the starting point for the first stitch. The little boy's hair is the best place to begin.

To work the stitches

1. Separate the strands of embroidery floss.
2. Rejoin three strands of floss, approximately 18 inches long, and thread your needle.
3. Follow the chart to determine where each stitch in each color is placed. Finish the design before beginning the letters.
4. When stitching the letters, check your place often to be sure it corresponds to the chart. The letters should be evenly spaced, as indicated. All solid, straight lines on the chart indicate a black outline, except along the legs, which are outlined with brown floss. Use a backstitch in the outline areas.
5. When you have finished the cross stitch, remove the tape from all edges.
6. Place the work face down on a padded ironing board and steam press.

To finish

1. Trim the excess Aida cloth around the design so it fits your frame, with an extra inch all around.
2. With the cross stitch face down, center the backing from the frame on the back of the work.
3. Pull the fabric to the back and tape it with the masking tape. (See p. xiii for framing directions.)
4. Check the front of the design as you do this to be sure you aren't distorting the picture.
5. Place finished work in the frame and hang.

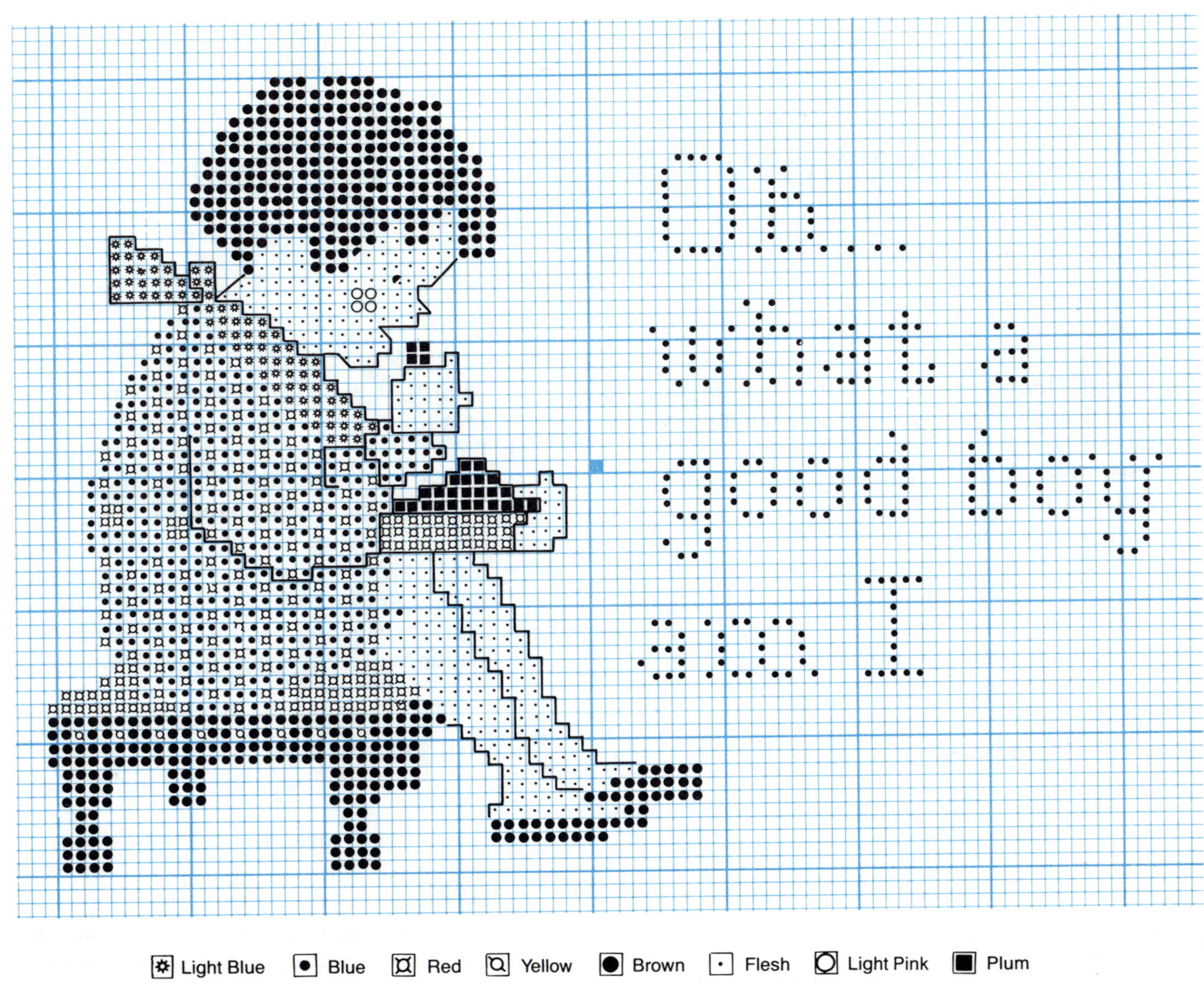

LITTLE JACK HORNER

Color key	DMC #
Light Blue	813
Blue	979
Red	350
Yellow	727
Brown	839
Flesh	945
Light Pink	818
Plum	3687

Outline of legs—Brown
Outline—face, arms, hands and dish—Black

Each square equals 1 stitch

FIRST DAY OF SPRING PILLOW

This charming little creature is enjoying the first whiff of spring. This is one of my favorite designs, which is worked on a pink and white Hopscotch Aida cloth from Charles Craft. Make the pillow for a new baby's room, to give to a teenager or to place on a summer porch. It is light and whimsical, and the full eyelet and dotted Swiss ruffles make it pretty and feminine. The finished pillow is 14 × 14 inches without the ruffles.

Materials

14-count white and pink Hopscotch Aida, 14 × 14 inches
embroidery floss in colors indicated on chart
needle
hoop
1½ yards of pregathered 2-inch-wide eyelet
strip of white dotted Swiss, 3 × 56 inches (can be pieced)
pink printed fabric 14½ × 14½ inches for backing
polyester stuffing or 14-inch pillow form
masking tape

Directions

1. Begin by binding all raw edges of the Aida cloth with masking tape.
2. Using the charted design provided, find the center square, which is solid.
3. Count the number of squares up and out from that point to the beginning of the first line of the charted design.
4. Find the center of the fabric by folding it in half vertically, then horizontally.
5. Each square on the graph corresponds to a square on your fabric. Since they are not always the same size, you count but do not measure.
6. Find the starting point for the first stitch, which will be the top of the flower.

To work the stitches

1. Separate the strands of embroidery floss.
2. Rejoin two strands of floss, approximately 18 inches long, and thread your needle.
3. With the Aida secured in the embroidery hoop, begin stitching the pink area of the flower. Continue with this color, filling in all the dark pink area as indicated on the chart. Remember to skip over the squares that will be filled with light pink and yellow floss.
4. When finished, place the work face down on a padded ironing board and steam press.
5. Remove tape from all edges.

To assemble pillow top

1. With right sides facing and raw edges aligned, pin the white eyelet around the outside edges of the stitched Aida so the ruffles lay flat on the cloth.
2. Machine stitch all around.

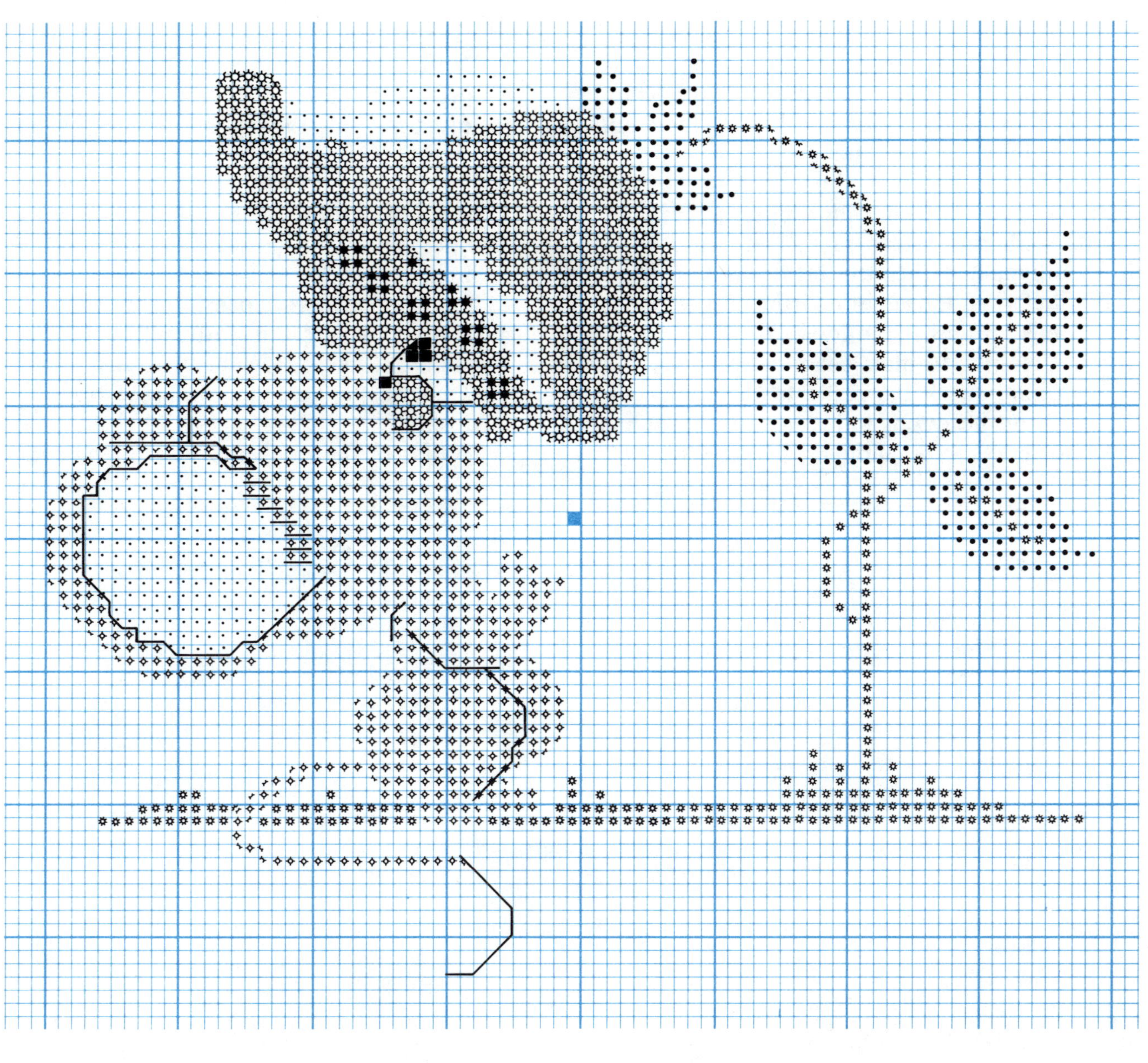

Dark Pink · Light Pink · Light Green · Dark Green · Yellow · Black · Light Brown

FIRST DAY OF SPRING PILLOW	**Color key**	**DMC #**
	Dark Pink	893
	Light Pink	776
	Light Green	471
	Dark Green	905
	Yellow	444
	Dark Brown	780
	Light Brown	437
	Outline—Dark Brown	780

Each square equals 1 stitch

3. With right sides facing, join short ends of the fabric strip to form a loop.
4. Turn one raw edge under 1/4 inch and press. Turn under another 1/4 inch and stitch to make a hem.
5. Divide the fabric into four equal parts and mark each with a pin.
6. With right sides facing and raw edges aligned, gather the fabric as you pin it between these points from corner to corner around the pillow.
7. Using a 1/4-inch seam allowance, machine stitch the ruffle to the pillow top from the wrong side, using the previous stitches as a guide.

To finish pillow

1. With right sides facing and raw edges aligned, pin the backing fabric to the pillow top with the eyelet and ruffle between.
2. From the wrong side, machine stitch the backing to the pillow top around three sides and four corners, leaving a few inches open for turning.
3. Trim the corners close to seam line.
4. Turn right side out and pull eyelet and ruffle out as you do this.
5. Press on the wrong side. Press ruffle all around.
6. Stuff and slipstitch the opening closed.

LITTLE CRITTERS WITH DAISY CHAIN

Here we have Mama Mouse with her baby holding a daisy chain and framed with pink floral fabric. Place this 10 × 15–inch picture in a pastel frame and hang in a child's room. The surrounding fabric matte can be made in a color to match the other elements in the room. Perhaps you have fabric to match the curtains or baby's crib quilt. This is a nice way to tie together all the accessories.

Materials

11-count white Aida cloth, 9 × 15 inches
embroidery floss in colors indicated on chart
needle
hoop
1/4 yard of printed fabric for matte
cardboard backing
masking tape

Directions

1. Begin by binding all raw edges of the Aida cloth with masking tape.
2. Using the charted design provided, find the center square, which is solid.
3. Count the number of squares up and out from that point to the beginning of the first line of the charted design.
4. Find the center of your fabric by folding it in half vertically, then horizontally.
5. Each square on the graph corresponds to a square on your fabric. Since they are not always the same size, you count but do not measure.
6. Find the starting point for the first stitch. You may want to start with the baby mouse, then the daisy chain up to Mama Mouse's skirt, then work the mouse before finishing the chain. Or another way to proceed could be to stitch each daisy in the center, then position the mice on each end. Plan how you will work before starting.

To work the stitches

1. Separate the strands of embroidery floss.
2. Rejoin three strands of floss, approximately 18 inches long, and thread your needle.
3. Follow the chart to determine where each stitch in each color is placed.
4. The mice are outlined with black floss, as indicated by straight, solid lines on the chart. The flowers are outlined in pink. All straight outlines are done with a backstitch.
5. When you have finished the cross stitch, remove the tape from all edges.
6. Place the work face down on a padded ironing board and steam press.

To finish

1. Trim the Aida cloth to measure 7 × 12 1/2 inches.
2. Cut two strips of fabric 2 1/2 × 15 1/2

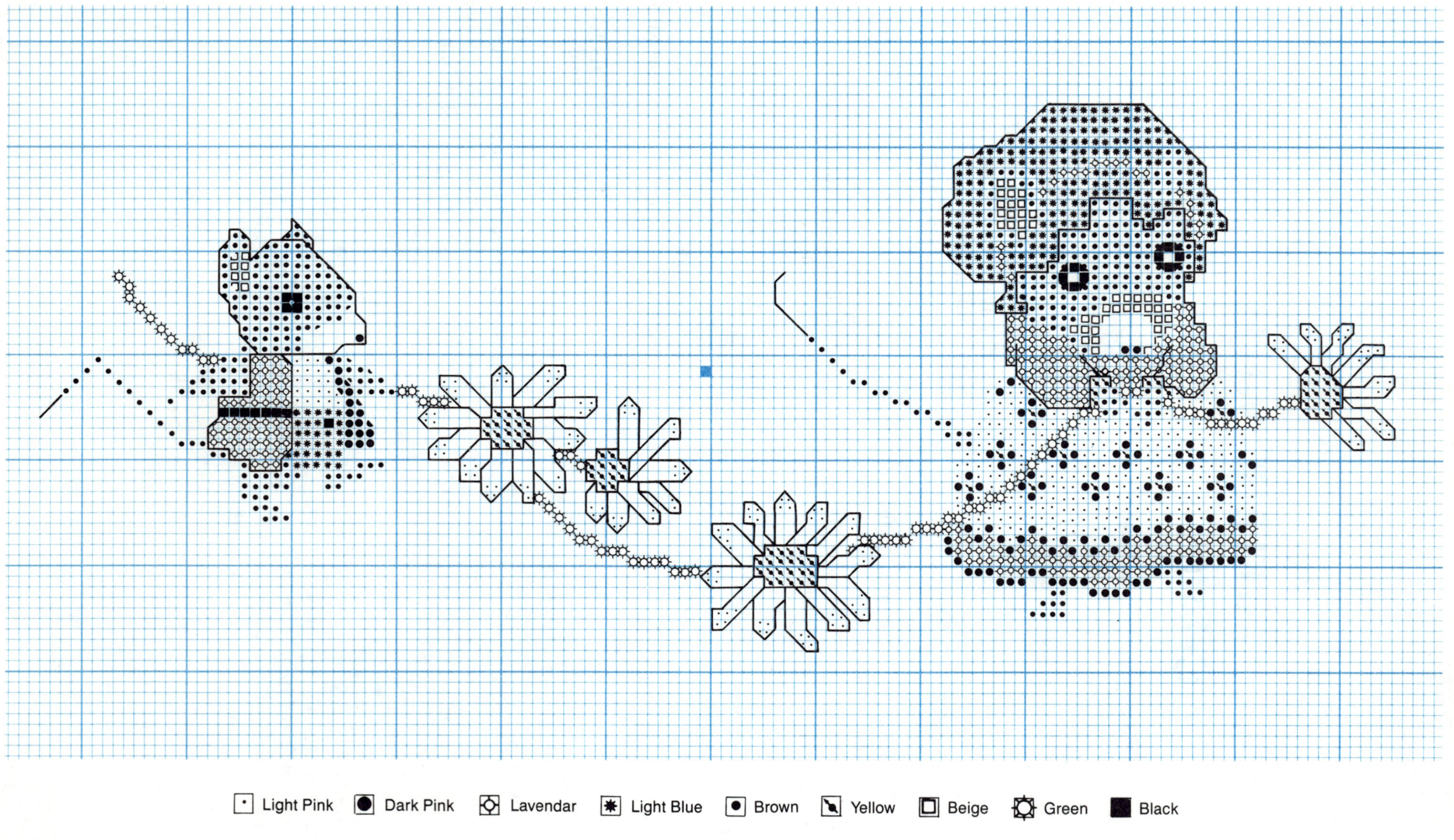
Light Pink
Dark Pink
Lavendar
Light Blue
Brown
Yellow
Beige
Green
Black

LITTLE CRITTERS WITH DAISY CHAIN

Color key	DMC #
Light Pink	776
Dark Pink	961
Lavender	210
Light Blue	747
Brown	435
Yellow	727
Beige	738
Green	704
Black	
Outline—Black	

Each square equals 1 stitch

inches. Cut two strips of fabric $2^1/_2 \times 7^1/_2$ inches.

3. With right sides facing and raw edges aligned, stitch one short strip of fabric to one side edge of the finished cross stitch piece, leaving $^1/_4$-inch seam allowance.
4. Open seams and press. Repeat on the opposite edge.
5. With right sides facing and raw edges aligned, stitch the long strips to the top and bottom edges of the cross stitch. Open seams and press.
6. With the cross stitch face down on the cardboard backing, tape all edges at the back with masking tape. (See p. xiii for framing directions.)
7. Check the front of the design to be sure you aren't distorting the picture as you tape it. Place in frame and hang.

GIRL IN A SWING

This is one of my favorite illustrations. Isn't this a darling project for a child's room, a breakfast area, a hallway or a bathroom? I especially like it on a summer porch, where it adds to a carefree environment. A blue printed fabric to match the details in the picture is used in place of the usual matte that's included with a frame. The picture is also slightly padded from behind to add to the softness of the project. The finished cross stitch area measures 5½ × 7½ inches, but when it is bordered, it fits into a standard 8½ × 11–inch frame.

Materials

14-count ecru Aida cloth, 8 × 10 inches
embroidery floss in colors indicated on chart
needle
hoop
thin quilt batting, 7½ × 9½ inches
printed fabric for border
frame, 8½ × 11 inches
masking tape

Directions

1. Begin by binding all raw edges of the Aida cloth with masking tape.
2. Using the charted design provided, find the center square, which is solid.
3. Count the number of squares up and out from that point to the beginning of the first line of the charted design.
4. Find the center of your fabric by folding it in half vertically, then horizontally.
5. Each square on the graph corresponds to a square on your fabric. Since they are not always the same size, you count but do not measure.
6. Find the starting point for the first stitch. For this project you may want to begin with the girl's hair, filling in the cloud outline after the picture is complete. Count down to this square to begin.

To work the stitches

1. Separate the strands of embroidery floss.
2. Rejoin two strands of floss, approximately 18 inches long, and thread your needle.
3. Follow the chart to determine where each stitch in each color is placed. The solid, straight lines on the chart indicate areas to be outlined in brown. These are always backstitches. There are many outline stitches on this project. Do these after the project has been completed.

GIRL IN A SWING

Color key	DMC #
Green	955
Blue	3325
Brown	780
Pink	818
Yellow	743
Flesh	945
Dark Pink	892
Outline—Brown	

Each square equals 1 stitch

Green · Blue · Brown · Pink · Yellow · Flesh · Dark Pink

4. When you have finished the cross stitch, remove the tape from all edges.
5. Place the cross stitch face down on a padded ironing board and steam press.

To finish

1. Trim the Aida cloth to measure 6 × 8 inches.
2. Cut two strips of printed fabric to 2 × 11½ inches. Cut two strips of printed fabric to 2 × 6 inches.
3. With right sides facing and raw edges aligned, stitch one short strip of fabric to the top edge of the Aida cloth. Open seams and press.
4. Repeat on the bottom edge.
5. With right sides facing and raw edges aligned, stitch the long strips to each side edge of the Aida. Open seams and press.
6. Place the quilt batting over the cardboard backing of the frame and center the cross stitch over it. Pull the fabric edges around to the back and tape securely all around. (See p. xiii for framing directions.)
7. Set the picture into the frame and hang.

PLATE 7 Vegetable Sampler, Cheerful Cherries, Flower Place Mat

PLATE 8 Home Sweet Home Sampler, Violet Pillow, Eyeglass Case

PLATE 9 Trio of Fruit, Summer Coasters

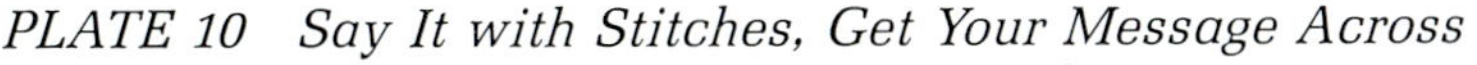
PLATE 10 Say It with Stitches, Get Your Message Across

PLATE 11   Welcome Sampler, Wild Duck Scene, Cardinal Pillow

PLATE 12   Wedding Monogram Pillow, Summer Scene Pillow, Delicate Napkin Rings, Mini Sachets, Towel Edging

Book Two

First Steps in Counted Cross Stitch

Home Accessories

FLOWER PLACE MAT

Make one special place mat or make a set of four. The single floral design running up one side of the fabric is pretty and dramatic, leaving plenty of room to set a place without covering the stitching. The calico border matches the green stems, but you might use a fabric color that goes with your decor. Since the Aida cloth, the calico and the floss are all cotton, you can throw the mats into the washer with no trouble. I would suggest air- rather than machine-drying to avoid shrinkage. The finished place mat is 12 × 16 inches.

Materials

14-count ecru Aida cloth, 12 × 16 inches
embroidery floss in colors indicated on chart
needle
hoop
1/2 yard of green calico
masking tape

Directions

1. Begin by binding all raw edges of the Aida cloth with masking tape.
2. Use the charted design provided to determine where the stitches will be placed. The top of the flower design starts approximately 2 1/2 inches from the left-hand edge of the Aida fabric and approximately 1 1/2 inches down from the top edge.
3. Each square on the graph corresponds to a square on your fabric. Find your starting point for the first stitch.

To work the stitches

1. Separate the strands of embroidery floss.
2. Rejoin two strands of floss, approximately 18 inches long, and thread your needle.
3. With the Aida cloth secured in the embroidery hoop, begin stitching the green areas, skipping over the squares that will later be filled in with pink floss.
4. Continue to work with the green floss, beginning and ending each length of thread as per directions on p. x.
5. When you have finished with the green areas, fill in all pink flowers, with the yellow centers worked last. Remove tape from edges.
6. When finished, place the work face down on a padded ironing board and steam press.

To make place mat

1. Cut the green calico to 13 × 17 inches.
2. With wrong sides facing, position the finished Aida cloth on the calico backing so there is 1 inch of calico all around.

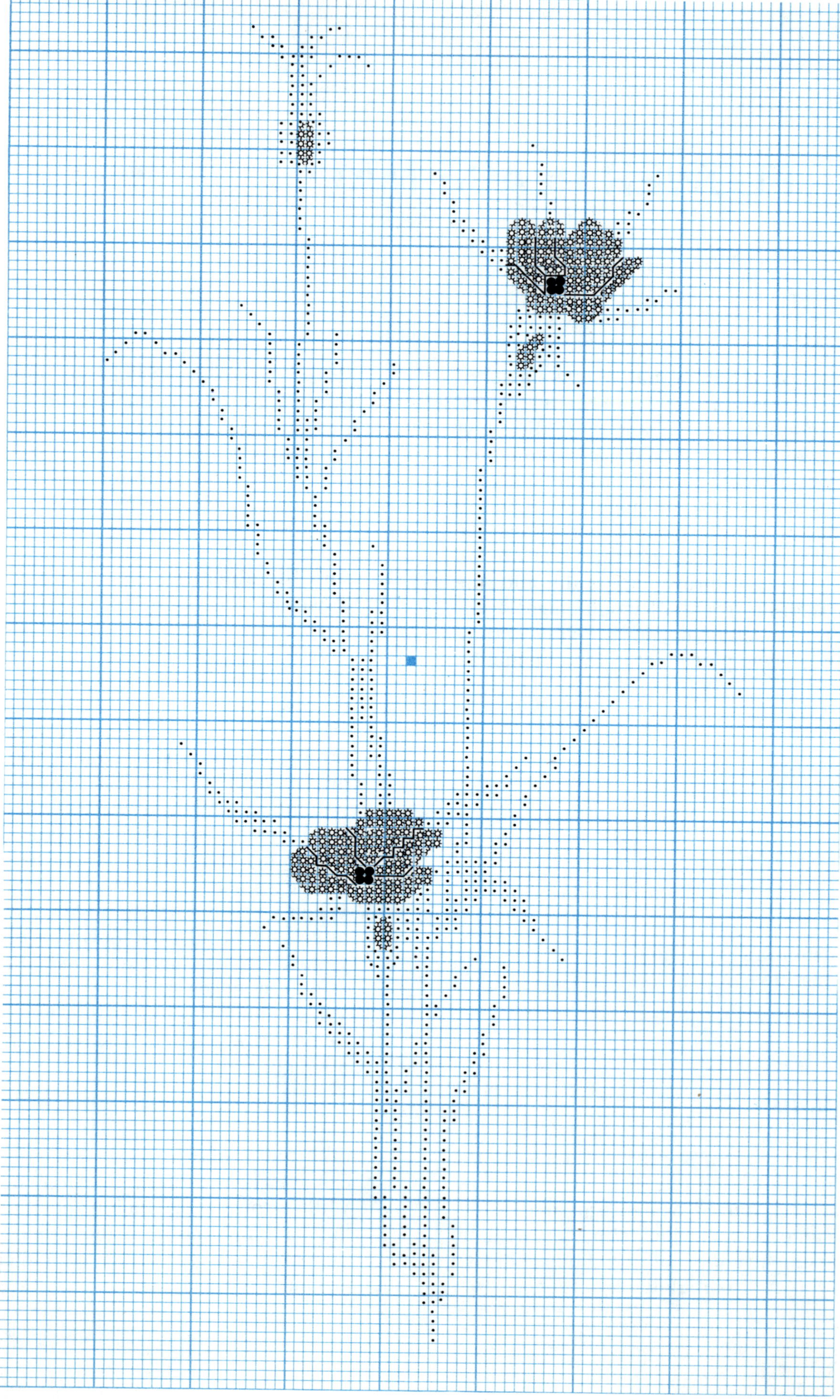

Pink

Green

Yellow

FLOWER PLACE MAT

Color key	DMC #
Pink	892
Green	911
Yellow	307

Each square equals 1 stitch

3. Turn the raw edges of the calico forward 1/4 inch and press.
4. Fold the remaining fabric forward, over the edge of the Aida, and pin it evenly all around on the front of the Aida cloth.
5. Using the same color thread, slipstitch or machine stitch all around close to the edge.
6. Turn the finished place mat face down on your ironing board and steam press.

TRIO OF FRUIT

A trio of framed fruit can be arranged on a tabletop or hung in a group to add cheer in a breakfast nook or dining area. Or consider using the designs for sachets, miniature pillows filled with potpourri or as pincushions. If you extend the background you can enlarge the overall size for any purpose. The finished picture area of the cherries is 3 × 3 inches, the pear is 3½ × 5 inches and the apple is 4½ × 4½ inches. These are wonderful quick-and-easy projects for all-occasion gifts.

Materials

CHERRIES: 11-count white Aida cloth, 6 × 6 inches
PEAR: 14-count red Aida cloth, 6 × 8 inches
APPLE: 14-count yellow Aida cloth, 6 × 6 inches
embroidery floss in colors indicated on charts
needle
hoop
matte and frame for each project
masking tape

Directions (for all three projects)

1. Begin by binding all raw edges of the Aida cloth with masking tape.
2. Using the charted designs provided, find the center square, which is solid.
3. Count the number of squares up and out from that point to the beginning of the first line of the charted designs.
4. Find the center of your fabric by folding it in half vertically, then horizontally.
5. Each square on the graph corresponds to a square on your fabric. Since they are not always the same size, you count but do not measure.
6. Find the starting point for the first stitch. Even though there is a background pattern of stitches on the pear and apple projects, you will work the fruit first, filling in the colored red or green background stitches last.

To work the stitches

1. Separate the strands of embroidery floss.
2. Rejoin three strands of floss for the cherry design, approximately 18 inches long, and thread your needle.
3. For the pear and apple design, you will use two strands of floss, since the Aida cloth is 14 count, rather than 11 count as for the cherries.
4. Follow the charts to determine where each stitch in each color is placed.
5. When you have finished the cross stitch, remove the tape from all edges.
6. Place the cross stitch face down on a padded ironing board and steam press.

To finish

1. Trim the excess Aida cloth around the design to the size of each frame.
2. Place the matte over the front of the project and frame for hanging. (See p. xiii for framing directions.)

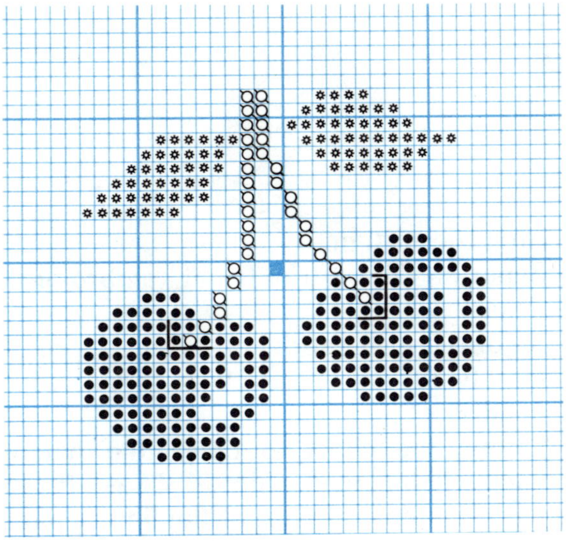

Black   Green   Red

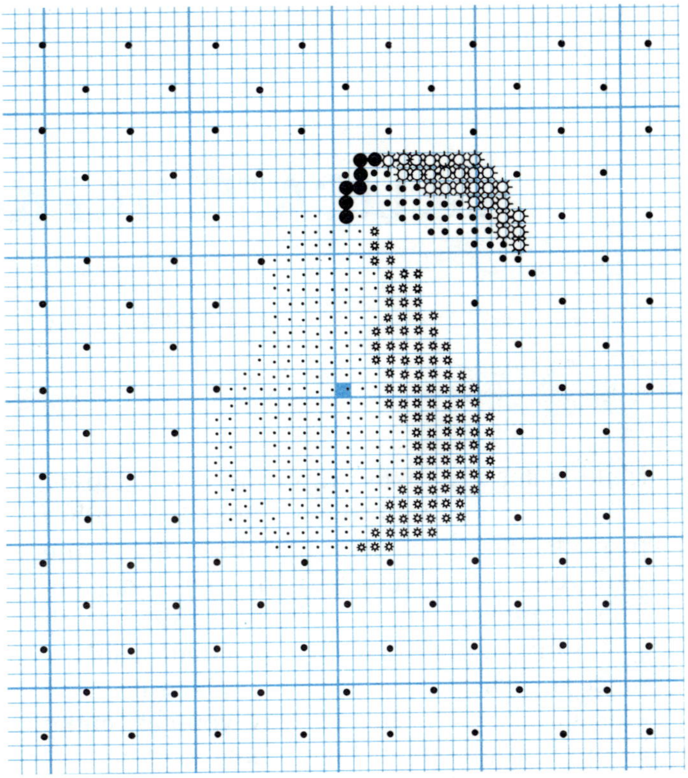

Yellow   Beige   Dark Green   Light Green   Brown

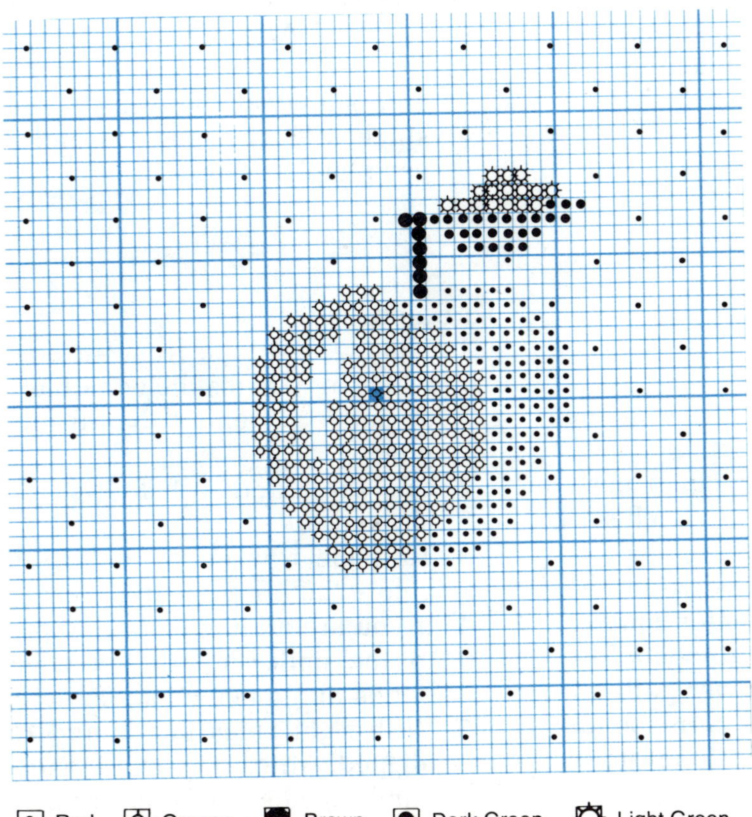

Red   Orange   Brown   Dark Green   Light Green

TRIO OF FRUIT

Color key	DMC #
Cherries	
Black	
Green	702
Red	666
Pear	
Yellow	444
Beige	437
Dark Green	699
Light Green	703
Brown	632
Apple	
Red	666
Orange	608
Brown	632
Dark Green	699
Light Green	703

Each square equals 1 stitch

DELICATE NAPKIN RINGS

Make a set of napkin rings from your leftover Aida cloth and embroidery floss from other projects. Slip a colorful napkin in each ring and you have a nice gift for any occasion. These rings require a piece of Aida cloth 1 × 5 inches for each. I've specified a larger piece to work with so you can place it in the embroidery hoop. In this way you can make several and then cut them apart to sew.

Materials (for four rings)

14-count white Aida cloth, 8 × 8 inches
embroidery floss in colors indicated on chart
needle
hoop
lace trim (optional)
masking tape

Directions

1. Begin by binding all raw edges of the cloth with masking tape.
2. Divide the fabric into four equal parts and mark lightly with a pencil. Each section will be 2 inches wide.
3. Count the number of squares within the 2-inch band and find the center square.
4. Using the charted design provided, find the center square of the flower pattern.
5. Each square on the graph corresponds to a square on your fabric. Count up to find the first stitch placement.

To work the stitches

1. Separate the strands of embroidery floss.
2. Rejoin two strands of floss, approximately 18 inches long, and thread your needle.
3. Follow the chart to determine where each stitch in each color is placed. Begin with the pink stitches of the flower part. You can complete each flower, changing to green floss, or stitch all the pink flowers, then all the green stems.
4. Space each flower evenly across the bands of Aida cloth.
5. There is a spacing of two rows above and below each flower. A border of red stitches finishes the top and bottom of each napkin ring.

To finish

1. Remove the tape from all edges of the Aida cloth. Place the work face down on a padded ironing board and steam press.
2. Cut the bands of fabric along your marked lines.
3. Turn the raw edges under, above and below the borders, and press.
4. If you are adding lace trim, pin the lace to the underside of the edges of the bands and machine stitch across.
5. With right sides facing and raw edges aligned, stitch the short ends of each band together to form a ring.

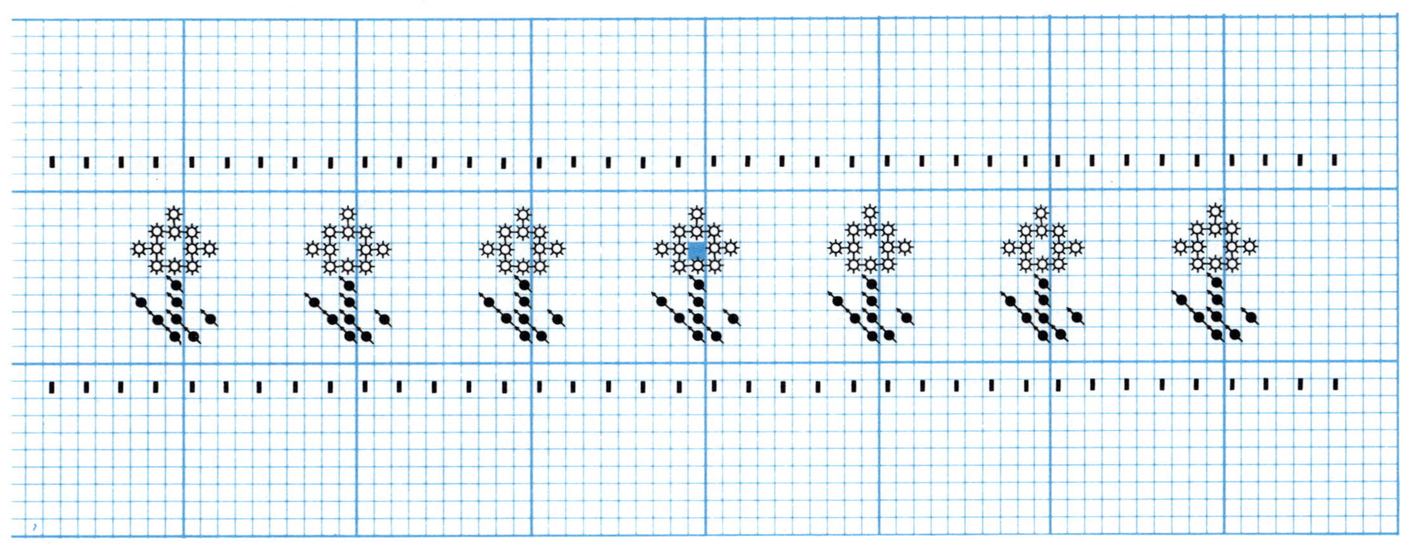

Green

Pink

Red

DELICATE NAPKIN RINGS

Color key	**DMC #**
Green	993
Pink	776
Red	309

Each square equals 1 stitch

TOWEL EDGING

Decorate plain towels with a band of cross stitch flowers and see how elegant they become. This is a good way to turn an ordinary gift into something special. Add a wide lace eyelet trim for an extra effect and you'll have a terrific wedding present.

Materials

14-count white Aida cloth, 3 inches × the length needed
embroidery floss in colors indicated on chart
needle
hoop
masking tape
white eyelet (optional)

Directions

1. Begin by binding all raw edges of the Aida cloth with masking tape.
2. Using the charted design provided, find the center square, which is solid.
3. Count the number of squares up and out from that point to the beginning of the first line of the charted design.
4. Find the center of your fabric by folding it in half vertically, then horizontally.
5. Each square on the graph corresponds to a square on your fabric. Since they are not always the same size, you count but do not measure.

To work the stitches

1. Separate the strands of embroidery floss.
2. Rejoin two strands of floss, approximately 18 inches long, and thread your needle.
3. Follow the chart to determine where each stitch in each color is placed. There is one space between each flower design and each stem of the next flower. Keep repeating the design all the way across your Aida strip.

To finish

1. Remove the tape from all edges and place the work face down on a padded ironing board. Steam press.
2. Turn the raw edges of the Aida strip under so that the design is centered on the strip. Press.
3. Place this in position on the towel and machine stitch along all edges.
4. Add the eyelet if desired.

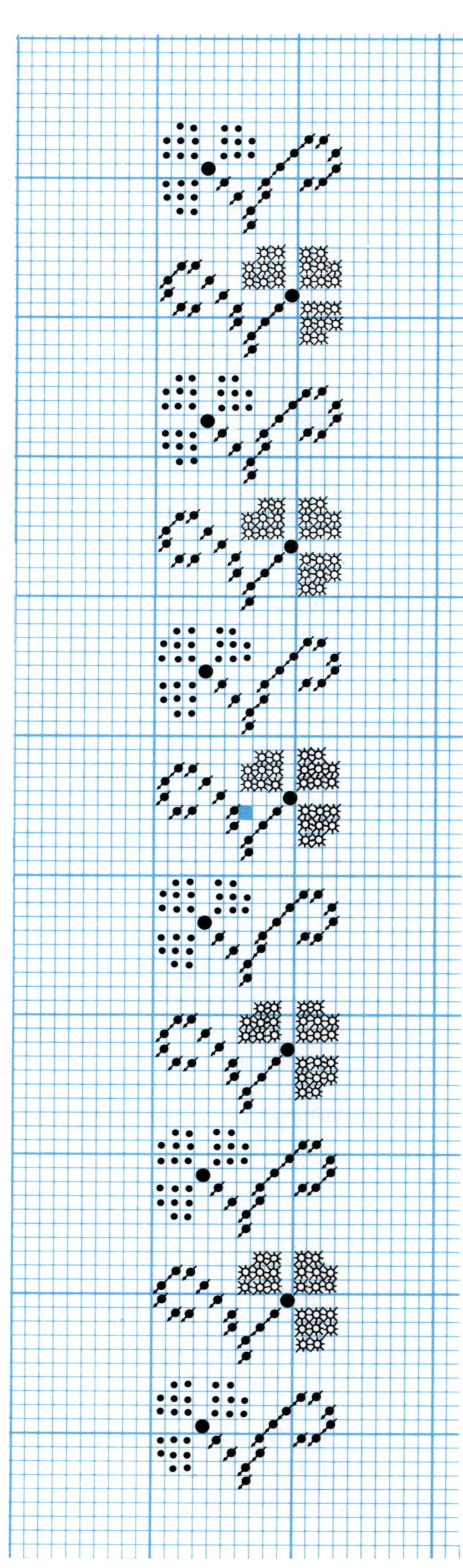

Pink

Blue

Green

Yellow

TOWEL EDGING

Color key	DMC #
Pink	892
Blue	793
Green	913
Yellow	307

Each square equals 1 stitch

SUMMER COASTERS

You can purchase a set of coasters made specially for crafting. The ones used here have a green plastic rim and a clear plastic inset, under which you insert your finished cross stitch, which you cut to size after stitching. They come in sets of four and in different colors. The three shown here are designed with summertime fruit slices of lime, watermelon and orange and are quick and easy projects. Each coaster is 3 inches in diameter.

Materials

14-count white Aida (a 5–6 inch square for each coaster)
embroidery floss in colors indicated on chart
needle
hoop
coasters
masking tape

Directions

1. Begin by binding all raw edges of the Aida cloth with masking tape.
2. Using the charted design provided, find the center square, which is solid.
3. Count the number of squares up and out from that point to the beginning of the first line of the charted design.
4. Find the center of your fabric by folding it in half vertically, then horizontally.
5. Each square on the graph corresponds to a square on your fabric. Since they are not always the same size, you count but do not measure.
6. Find the starting point for the first stitch. When making the coaster with the watermelon design, notice on the finished project that the fruit is placed at the bottom rather than in the middle of the fabric. Start the stitching with enough fabric above it to fill the coaster. There should be approximately 20 lines above and 5 lines below the finished design.

To work the stitches

1. Separate the strands of embroidery floss.
2. Rejoin two strands of floss, approximately 18 inches long, and thread your needle.
3. Follow the chart to determine where each stitch in each color is placed.

To finish

1. When you have finished the cross stitch, remove the tape from all edges and place the work face down on a padded ironing board. Steam press.
2. Use the plastic inset from the coaster to draw a circle around each design. Cut out and place in the coasters.

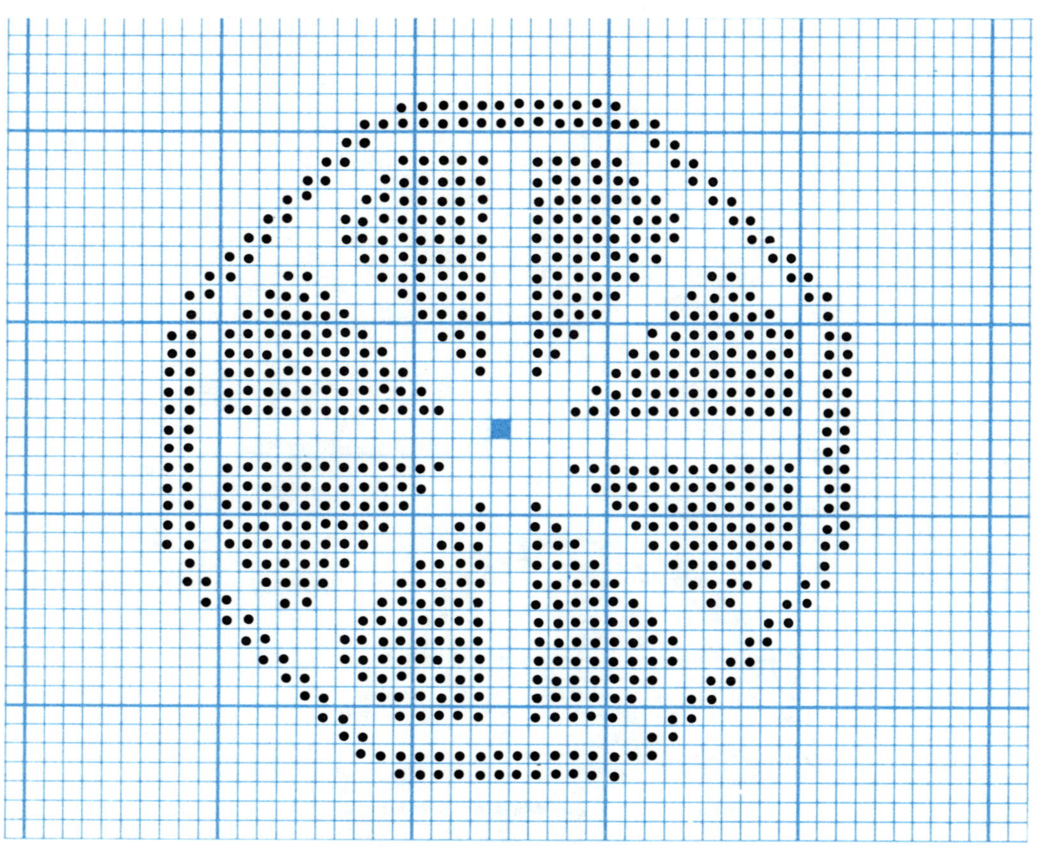

SUMMER COASTERS

Color key	DMC #
Orange	
Orange	740

Each square equals 1 stitch

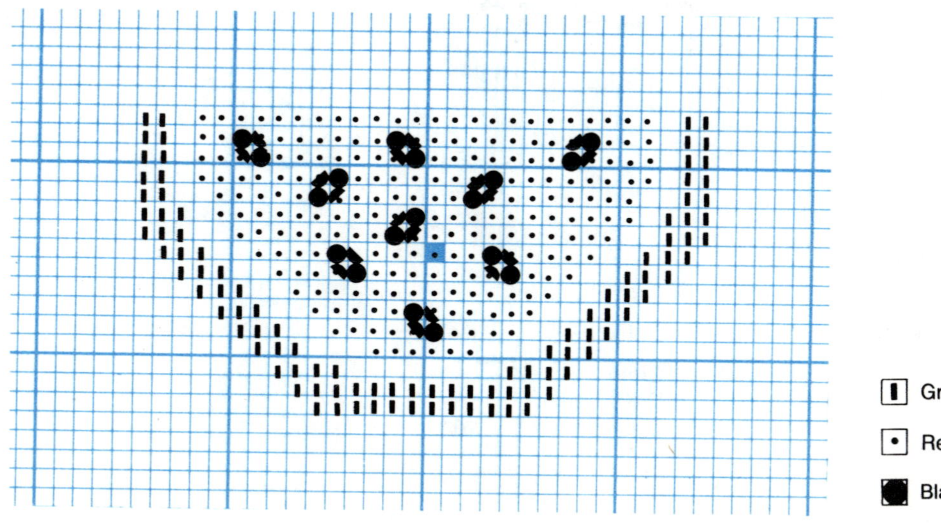

SUMMER COASTERS

Color key	DMC #
Watermelon	
Green	911
Red	606
Black	

Each square equals 1 stitch

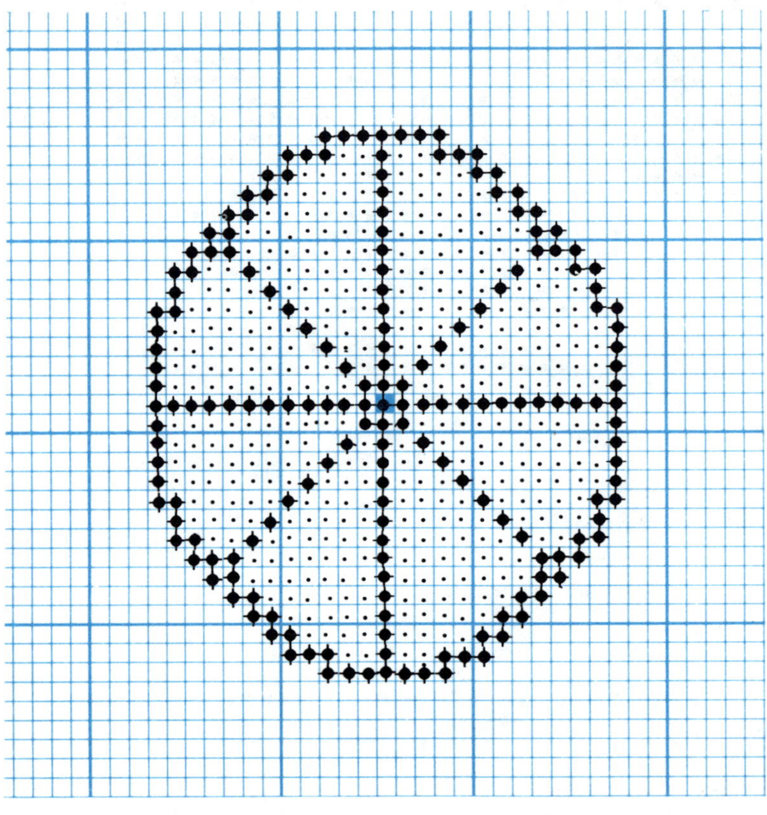

◆ Dark Green

· Light Green

SUMMER COASTERS	Color key	DMC #
	Lime	
	Dark Green	699
	Light Green	703

Each square equals 1 stitch

EYEGLASS CASE

A pretty eyeglass case is always a welcome gift. Make one that is personalized with your own or a friend's initials and surround them with a pretty border. This one has a nice geometric, tailored look. For a man, consider making it in dark colors, such as wine and navy blue or dark brown and burnt orange. The finished size is 3 × 6 inches.

Materials

14-count white Aida cloth, 6½ × 12½ inches
embroidery floss in colors indicated on chart
needle
hoop
printed fabric for lining
masking tape

Directions

1. Begin by taping all raw edges of the Aida.
2. Using the charted design provided, find the center square, which is solid.
3. Count the number of squares up and out from that point to the beginning of the first line, which will be solid on the chart.
4. Fold the fabric in half so you are working with a piece that is 3¼ × 6¼ inches. Find the center of this piece by folding it in half vertically, then horizontally.
5. Each square on the graph corresponds to a square on your fabric. Since they are not always the same size, you count but do not measure.
6. Find the starting point for the first stitch.

To work the stitches

1. Separate the strands of floss.
2. Rejoin two strands of floss, approximately 18 inches long, and thread your needle.
3. Follow the chart to determine where each stitch in each color is placed. You can work the entire border design and then do the initials, followed by the inner borders. Or you can work the initials first, finishing with each border as it surrounds the initials.
4. Check the letters to be sure they're evenly spaced, and count your squares accurately so that the borders meet properly at each corner.

To finish

1. Remove the tape from all edges and place the work face down on a padded ironing board. Steam press.
2. With right sides facing, fold the Aida cloth in half so the unstitched piece is on top of the cross stitch. Press.
3. Machine stitch along the long raw edge close to the cross stitched outside border. Stitch along the bottom, raw edge.
4. Trim away the excess fabric and turn right side out.
5. Turn the top edge to the inside and press.

EYEGLASS CASE

Color key	DMC #
Yellow	444
Blue	332
Green	988

Each square equals 1 stitch

Lining

1. Cut two pieces of printed fabric 3½ × 6½ inches.
2. With right sides facing and raw edges aligned, stitch along both sides and across the bottom edge, leaving a ¼-inch seam allowance.
3. Slip the lining inside the eyeglass case and turn the top, raw edge under so it is between the lining and outside case.
4. Slipstitch the lining and eyeglass case together around the top edge.

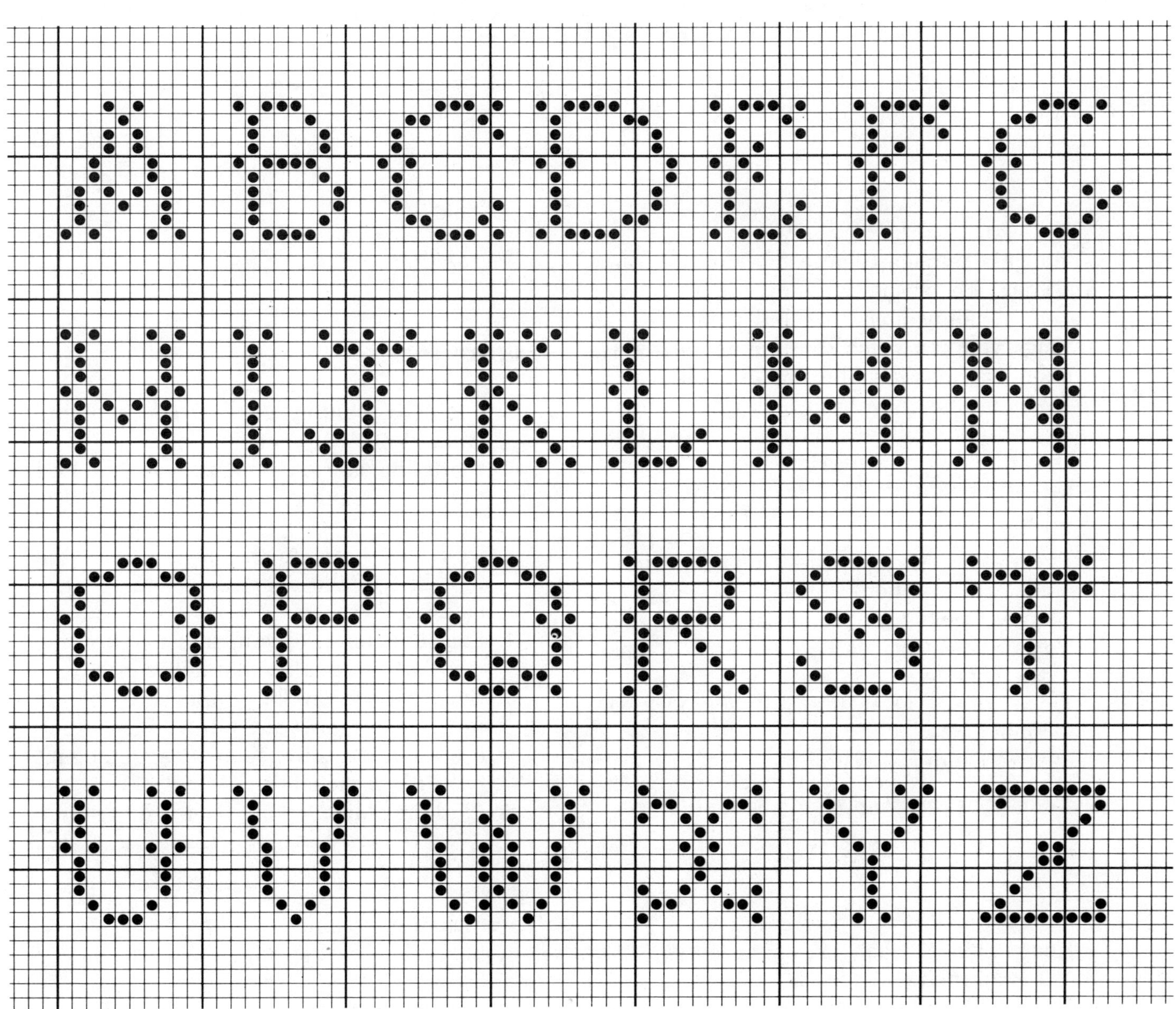

SAY IT WITH STITCHES

Keep This Kitchen Clean . . . Eat Out, May all your weeds be wildflowers and Love builds a happy home are but a few of the sayings you can stitch for hanging or giving. Stitched sayings have become a popular way to let everyone know your feelings in a decorative way. Sometimes they add a bit of humor to an environment. Here is a list of some others that you might prefer. They can be used with the borders provided here.

I'm Making My Favorite Thing for Dinner . . . Reservations
Skinny Cooks Can't Be Trusted
You Have 2 Choices For Dinner . . . Take It or Leave It
Once You're Over the Hill You Pick Up Speed
39 and Holding

Take your pick and say it with stitches!

Materials

Keep This Kitchen: 11-count ecru Aida, 9 × 12 inches
Love builds: 11-count white Aida, 8 × 10 inches
May all your weeds: 14-count fiddler's cloth, 8 × 12 inches
embroidery floss in colors indicated on charts
needle
hoop
frames and mattes
masking tape

Directions

1. Begin by binding all raw edges of the Aida cloth with masking tape.
2. Using the charted designs provided, find the center square, which is solid.
3. Count the number of squares up and out from that point to the beginning of the first line of the charted design you are using.
4. Find the center of your fabric by folding it in half vertically, then horizontally.
5. Each square on the graph corresponds to a square on your fabric. Since they are not always the same size, you count but do not measure.
6. Find the starting point for the first stitch.

To work the stitches

1. Separate the strands of embroidery floss.
2. Rejoin three strands if the project is on 11-count Aida and two strands if you are working on 14-count fiddler's cloth. Cut a length approximately 18 inches and thread your needle.
3. Follow the charts to determine where each stitch in each color is placed. Finish the saying before working the borders so you are sure the letters are centered.

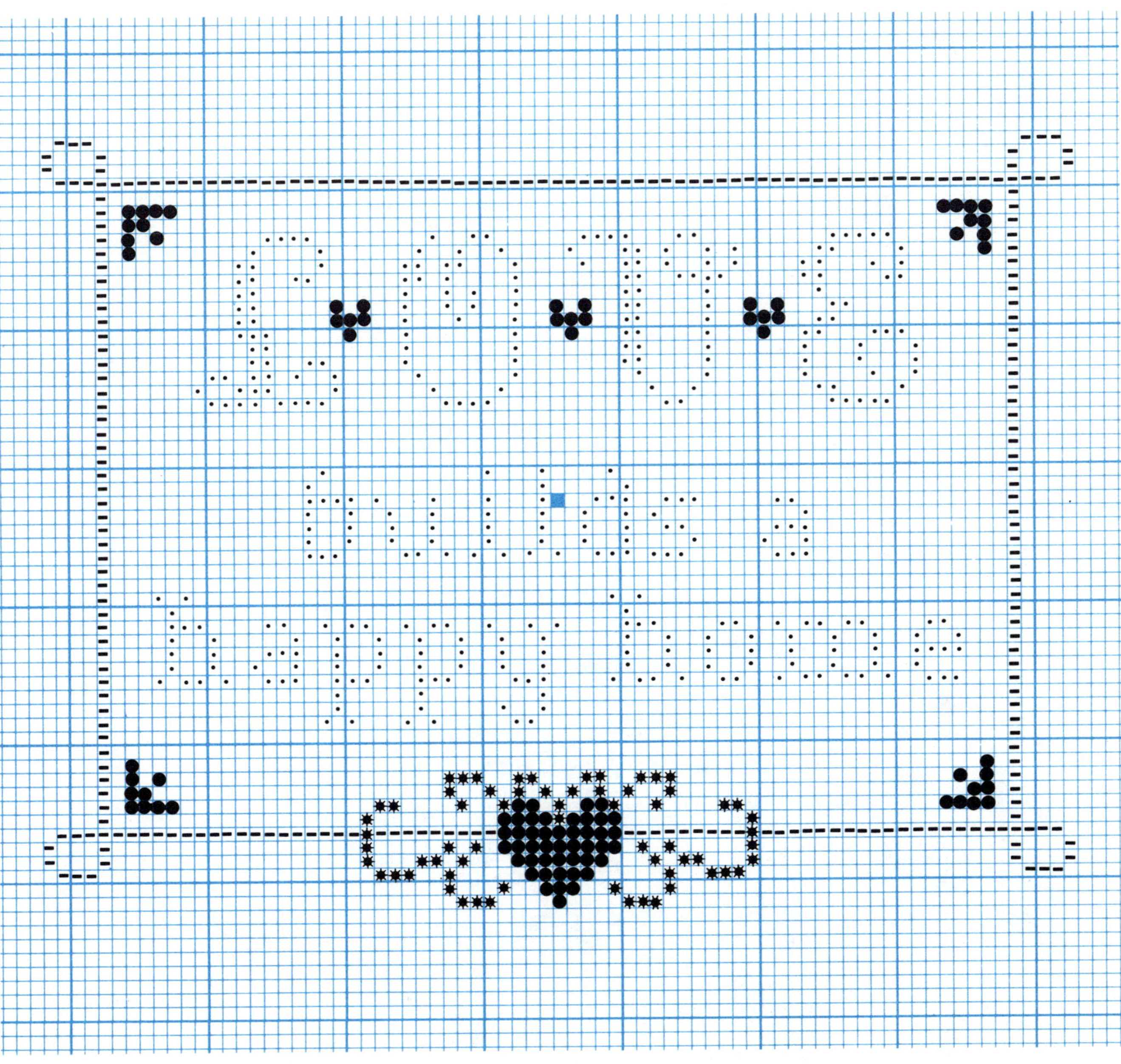

Blue   Yellow   Pink   Green

To finish

1. Remove the tape from all edges of the cloth.
2. Place the work face down on your padded ironing board and steam press.
3. Trim the Aida cloth around the saying so that it will fit the frame you are using.
4. Center the cross stitch on the backing, place the matte board on top and frame. (See p. xiii.)

SAY IT WITH STITCHES	**Color key**	**DMC #**
	Love builds a happy home	
	Blue	798
	Yellow	742
	Pink	603
	Green	911

Each square equals 1 stitch

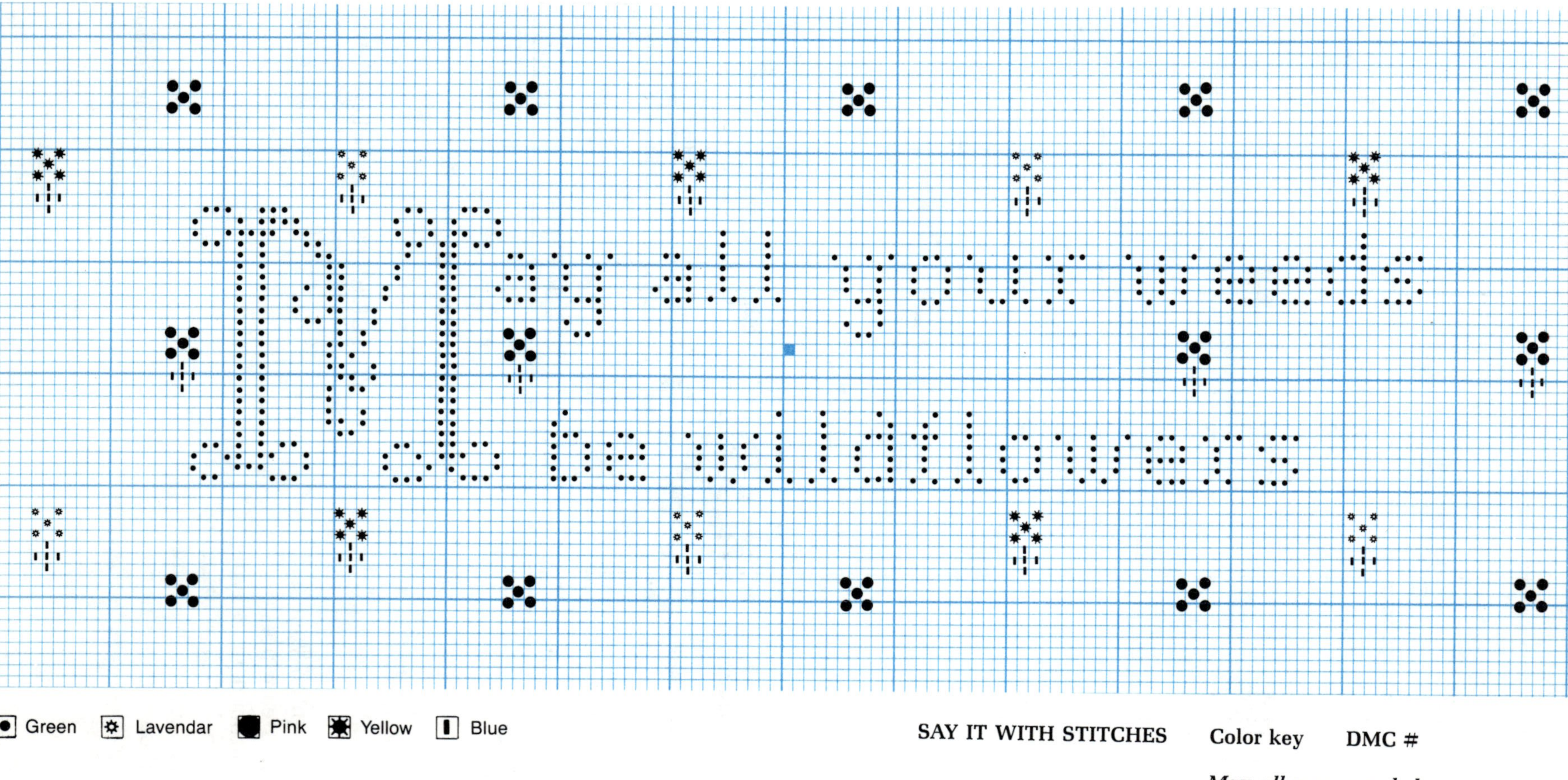

SAY IT WITH STITCHES

Color key	DMC #
May all your weeds be wildflowers	
Green	911
Lavender	553
Pink	603
Yellow	742
Blue	798

Each square equals 1 stitch

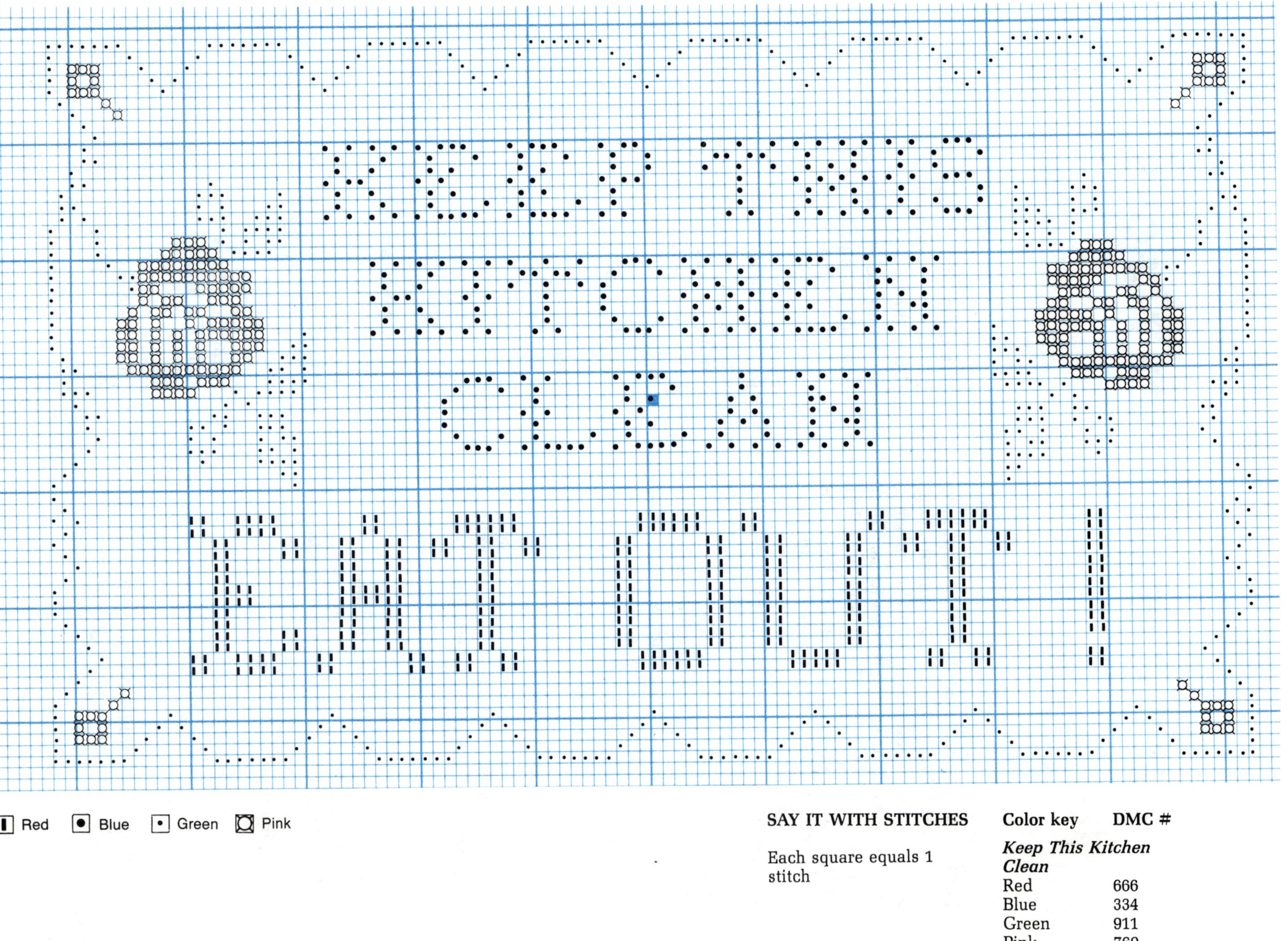

Red | Blue | Green | Pink

SAY IT WITH STITCHES

Each square equals 1 stitch

Color key	DMC #
Keep This Kitchen Clean	
Red	666
Blue	334
Green	911
Pink	760

GET YOUR MESSAGE ACROSS

Perhaps you're familiar with all the pillows and plaques that express a sentiment. Some are whimsical and fun and make us smile when a particular saying relates to us. These can be just the right gift for any occasion. This pillow says it for many of us: "When the going gets tough . . . the tough go shopping." It's a quick and easy design to work up, and you can finish it with a border of fabric in the color and pattern of your choice. Match the embroidery stitches to the fabric color and tuck it in a corner of the couch or in the family room. The finished pillow is 10 × 16 inches and the embroidered area is 4½ × 10½ inches.

Materials

- 11-count white Aida cloth, 8 × 14 inches
- embroidery floss in colors indicated on chart
- needle
- hoop
- ½ yard of printed fabric for borders and backing
- 1½ yards of pregathered 1-inch-wide eyelet
- masking tape

Directions

1. Begin by binding all raw edges of the Aida cloth with masking tape.
2. Using the charted design provided, find the center square, which is solid.
3. Count the number of squares up and out from that point to the beginning of the first line of the charted design.
4. Find the center of your fabric by folding it in half vertically, then horizontally.
5. Each square on the graph corresponds to a square on your fabric. Since they are not always the same size, you count but do not measure.
6. Find your starting point for the first stitch.

To work the stitches

1. Separate the strands of embroidery floss.
2. Join three strands of floss, approximately 18 inches long, and thread your needle.
3. Follow the chart to determine where each stitch in each color is placed.
4. Stop to check your place every so often. Check your stitches to be sure you haven't made an error. Remove tape from edges.
5. When finished, place the work face down on a padded ironing board and steam press.

To assemble pillow top

1. From the printed fabric, cut two border pieces 3½ × 11½ inches. Cut two pieces 3½ × 11½ inches.
2. Trim the Aida around the cross stitch so you have a piece 5 × 11½ inches.

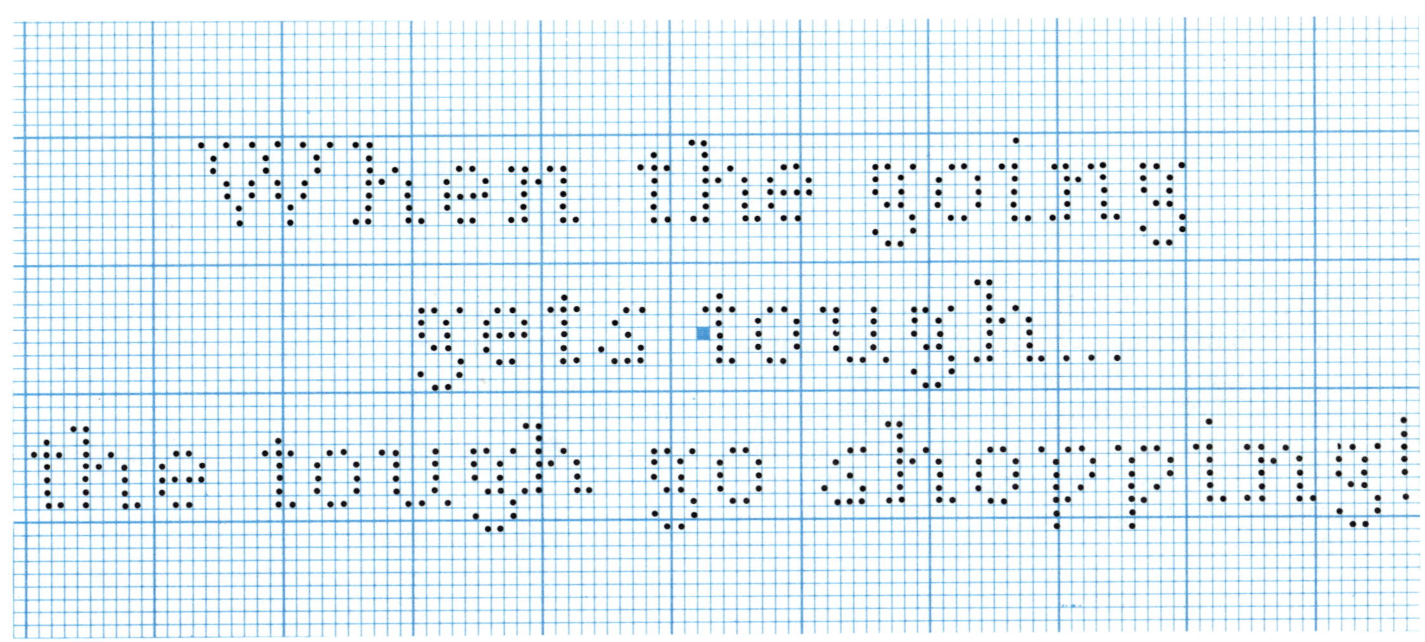

GET YOUR MESSAGE ACROSS	Color key	DMC #
	Pink	892
	Each square equals 1 stitch	

3. With right sides facing and raw edges aligned, stitch one $3\frac{1}{2} \times 11\frac{1}{2}$–inch fabric border along the top edge of the Aida, leaving a $\frac{1}{4}$-inch seam allowance.
4. Open seams and press. Repeat on the opposite side.
5. With right sides facing and raw edges aligned, join the remaining border pieces. Open seams and press.

To finish pillow

1. With right sides facing and raw edges aligned, pin the eyelet trim around all edges of the fabric. Machine stitch together, leaving a $\frac{1}{4}$-inch seam allowance.
2. Cut a piece of printed fabric $10\frac{1}{2} \times 16\frac{1}{2}$ inches for the backing.
3. With right sides facing and raw edges aligned, pin the backing to the pillow top, with the eyelet between.
4. Machine stitch all around three sides and four corners. Leave a few inches open for turning.
5. Clip corners and turn right side out. Press on the wrong side, not over the cross stitch.
6. Stuff until the pillow is nice and full. Slipstitch the opening closed.

MINI SACHETS

Fill a basket with our mini sachets and place in the bathroom or bring to a friend. These are lovely little gifts as well as bazaar best-sellers. Tuck one into a Christmas or birthday package for a sweet-smelling surprise. You can make a few in no time and fill with your favorite potpourri scent. They measure $2^1/_2 \times 3$ inches.

Materials

14-count white Aida cloth $5^1/_2 \times 7^1/_2$ inches for each sachet
embroidery floss in colors indicated on chart
needle
hoop
6 inches of lace for each
ribbon or rickrack for tying
masking tape

Directions

1. Begin by binding raw edges with masking tape.
2. Using the charted design provided, find the center square, which is solid.
3. Count the number of squares up and out from that point to the beginning of the first line, which will be the border on the charted design.
4. Find the center of your fabric by folding it in half vertically, then horizontally.
5. Each square on the graph corresponds to a square on your fabric. Since they are not always the same size, you count but do not measure.
6. Find the starting point for the first stitch.

To work the stitches

1. Separate the strands of floss.
2. Rejoin two strands of floss, approximately 18 inches long, and thread your needle.
3. Follow the chart to determine where each stitch in each color is placed. Since this is an overall pattern, you can make the sachet as large or small as you wish. Simply continue the design to make the sachet larger.

To finish

1. Remove the tape from the edges and place the work face down on a padded ironing board. Steam press.
2. With right sides facing, fold the Aida cloth in half so the unstitched Aida is on top of the cross stitched piece. Press.
3. Machine stitch along one side as close to the cross stitch as possible and along the bottom edge. Trim away the excess fabric and turn right side out.
4. Turn the top, raw edge under and press. Stitch the lace edging all around to finish off.
5. Add rickrack or ribbon if desired to pull the top closed. Fill with potpourri or a small item to give as a gift.

A:

Pink

Green

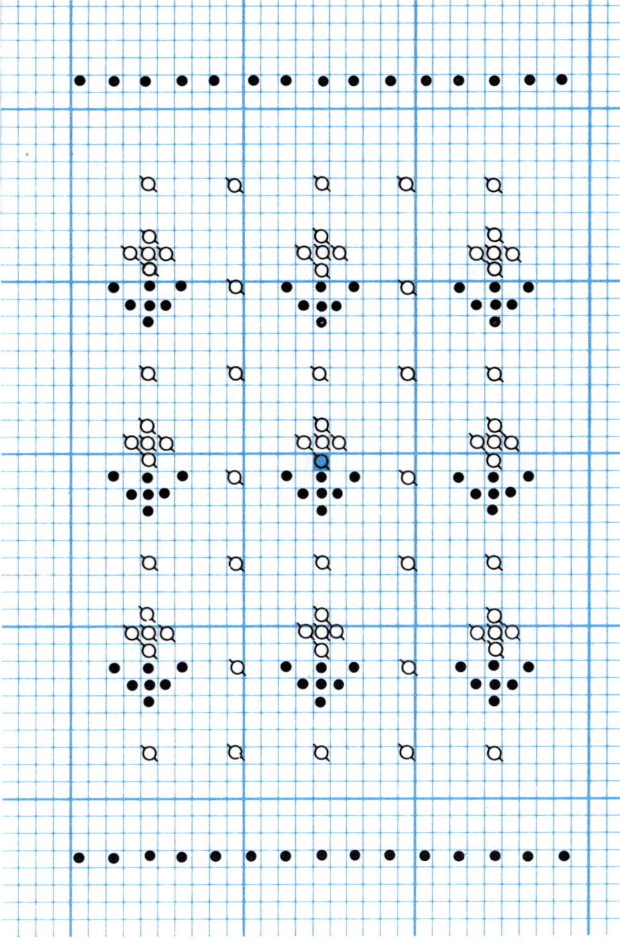

MINI SACHETS

Color key	DMC #
A: Pink	604
Green	913
B: Yellow	307
Green	913

Each square equals 1 stitch

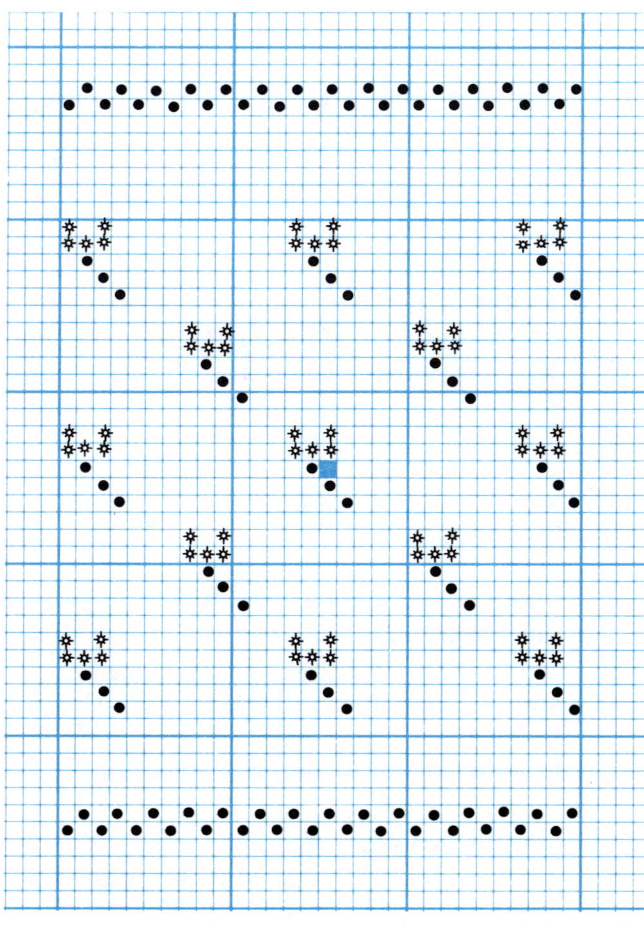

B:

Yellow

Green

VIOLET PILLOW

You can buy ready-made pillow shams with the front made of Aida cloth. The ruffles, backing and lace trim are part of the finished item. You simply cross stitch the front and stuff the pillow when finished. The opening is in the back, which is stitched closed after stuffing. You have a choice of different colored fabrics, sizes and shapes. It's an easy way to make a cross stitch project, because once the cross stitching is completed, there is no more sewing to do. This round pillow is approximately 12 inches in diameter without the ruffles.

Materials

14-count ecru Aida pillow sham
embroidery floss in colors indicated on chart
needle
hoop
polyester stuffing

Directions

1. Using the charted design provided, find the center square, which is solid.
2. Count the number of squares up and out from that point to the beginning of the first line of the charted design.
3. Find the center of the pillow by folding it in half vertically and then horizontally.
4. Each square on the graph corresponds to a square on the fabric. Since they are not always the same size, you count but do not measure.
5. Find the starting point for the first stitch.

To work the stitches

1. Separate the strands of embroidery floss.
2. Rejoin two strands of floss, approximately 18 inches long, and thread your needle.
3. Follow the chart to determine where each stitch in each color is placed. Finish the entire design before filling in the center squares of the flowers with yellow floss.

To finish

1. With the cross stitch face down on a padded ironing board, steam press on the wrong side. You have to press over the backing fabric, or reach the iron inside the opening of the back to press on the back of the Aida pillow front. If there are creases in the Aida, dampen the pillow backing and use it as a press cloth to iron the cross stitch.
2. Fill the pillow with stuffing and slipstitch the opening closed.

VIOLET PILLOW

Color key	DMC #
Green	319
Violet	552
Blue	793
Lavender	209
Yellow	307

Each square equals 1 stitch

WEDDING MONOGRAM PILLOW

This monogrammed pillow surrounded by green vines and roses makes a lovely wedding gift. Add to the cross stitched center a lavish trim of fabric piping, crocheted lace and a wide, full ruffle for an elegant gift that will surely become an heirloom. You might also consider this for an anniversary or christening gift as well.

When working on this project to give as a gift, I suggest that you work on the border stitches first, adding the initial in the center at the very end. In this way, should you fall in love with the project, you can always add your own initial instead of the one intended for a friend!

The finished pillow with a 3-inch ruffle is 15 × 15 inches. The cross stitched Aida pillow is about 9½ × 9½ inches.

Materials

14-count ecru Aida cloth, 12 × 12 inches
embroidery floss in colors indicated on chart
needle
hoop
1¼ yards of blue piping to match floss
strip of pink fabric 3½ × 60 inches (can be pieced)
printed blue fabric, 10 × 10 inches for backing
42 inches of pregathered 1-inch-wide lace
polyester stuffing
masking tape

Directions

1. Begin by binding all raw edges of the Aida cloth with masking tape.
2. Using the charted design provided, find the center square, which is solid.
3. Count the number of squares up and out from that point to the beginning of the first line of the charted design.
4. Find the center of the fabric by folding it in half vertically, then horizontally.
5. Each square on the graph corresponds to a square on your fabric. Since they are not always the same size, you count but do not measure.
6. Find your starting point for the first stitch.

To work the stitches

1. Separate the strands of embroidery floss.
2. Rejoin two strands of floss, approximately 18 inches long, and thread your needle.
3. With the Aida secured in the embroidery hoop, begin stitching the green leaves and vine. Continue with this color, filling in all green areas indicated on the chart. Or work the green stitches up to the first rose. Change to pink floss and stitch the roses. Then continue with the green vines, and finally the blue buds.
4. When you have finished the border,

Pink • Green ▮ Blue

WEDDING MONOGRAM PILLOW

Color key	DMC #
Pink	3326
Green	988
Blue	794

Each square equals 1 stitch

place the work face down on a padded ironing board and steam press.

5. Once again find the center of your fabric and count up and out to begin the first stitch of the monogram.
6. When finished, press as before. Remove tape from edges.

To assemble pillow top

1. Trim the Aida around the cross stitch so you have a piece 10 × 10 inches.
2. With right sides facing and raw edges aligned, pin the piping around the outside edges of the stitched Aida.
3. Machine stitch together with a 1/4-inch seam allowance.
4. Next, pin the lace around the edge as you did the piping.
5. From the wrong side, using the piping stitches as a guide, machine stitch the lace all around.
6. Pin the lace down over the Aida, especially at the corners to hold it out of the way while you add the fabric ruffle all around. This is simply a precaution so you don't catch the lace while stitching the ruffle and backing to the pillow.
7. Turn one long edge of the pink fabric strip under 1/4 inch and press. Turn under another 1/4 inch and press. Stitch the hem.
8. With right sides facing and raw edges aligned, stitch together the two short ends of the pink strip to form a loop.
9. Divide the fabric into four equal parts and mark each with a pin.
10. With right sides facing and raw edges aligned, gather the fabric as you pin it between these points from corner to corner around the pillow.
11. Flatten the ruffle on the pillow front and pin here and there to hold it away from the seam line. Using a 1/4-inch seam allowance, stitch the ruffle to the pillow top all around.

To finish pillow

1. With right sides facing and raw edges aligned, pin the backing fabric to the pillow top. The piping, lace and ruffle will be between.
2. From the wrong side, machine stitch the backing to the pillow, using the ruffle stitches as a guide. Stitch around three sides and four corners.
3. Trim the corners close to the seam line.
4. Turn right side out and pull lace and ruffle out as you do this. Press on wrong side. Press ruffle all around.
5. Stuff the pillow, making sure to fill each corner sufficiently. Slipstitch the opening closed.

CHEERFUL CHERRIES

Frame a simple bunch of cherries for a cheerful touch. This is a good example of a design that can be used for several projects. It can be framed, made into a pillow or used on a place mat. Matte and frame it to fit the area where it will be displayed. The finished cross stitch area is 5 × 7 inches and the overall framed object is 8½ × 10½ inches.

Materials

14-count ecru Aida, 7 × 9 inches
embroidery floss in colors indicated on chart
needle
hoop
frame and matte board
masking tape

Directions

1. Begin by binding all raw edges of the cloth with masking tape.
2. Using the charted design provided, find the center square, which is solid.
3. Count the number of squares up and out from that point to the beginning of the first line of the charted design.
4. Find the center of your fabric by folding it in half vertically, then horizontally.
5. Each square on the graph corresponds to a square on your fabric. Since they are not always the same size, you count but do not measure.
6. Find the starting point for the first stitch.

To work the stitches

1. Separate the strands of embroidery floss.
2. Rejoin two strands of floss, approximately 18 inches long, and thread your needle.
3. Follow the chart to determine where each stitch in each color is placed. With this design it is best to finish the leaves, then move on to the brown branch and then the green stems, and finally the cherries. In this way you are moving down the design according to color rather than across each line, which would necessitate changing colors in the middle or at the end of each line.

To finish

1. Remove the tape from all edges and place the work face down on a padded ironing board. Steam press.
2. Trim the Aida cloth around the design so it fits your frame.
3. Place the work over the backing board of the frame. Center the matte board and frame over the work and hang. (See p. xiii for framing details.)

Red Brown Dark Green Light Green

CHEERFUL CHERRIES

Color key	DMC #
Red	666
Brown	632
Dark Green	699
Light Green	703

Each square equals 1 stitch

VEGETABLE SAMPLER

You don't have to be a vegetarian to enjoy making and displaying this vegetable sampler. It is colorful and graphic and will look good in any kitchen, whether country or contemporary. Choose a matte board and frame to suit the area where it will hang. The finished project without matte is 8 × 10 inches.

Materials

14-count white Aida cloth, 10 × 14 inches
embroidery floss in colors indicated on chart
needle
hoop
frame and matte board
masking tape

Directions

1. Begin by taping all edges of the Aida cloth with masking tape.
2. Using the charted design provided, find the center square, which is solid.
3. Count the number of squares up and out from that point to the beginning of the first line of the border design.
4. Find the center of your fabric by folding it in half vertically, then horizontally.
5. Each square on the graph corresponds to a square on your fabric. Since they are not always the same size, you count but do not measure.
6. Find the starting point for the first stitch. Since the borders surround each fruit design, stitch them first so that each element will be accurately centered within its designated area.

To work the stitches

1. Separate the strands of embroidery floss.
2. Rejoin two strands of floss, approximately 18 inches long, and thread your needle.
3. Follow the chart to determine where each color is placed. Check your stitches often to be sure the corners of each border will meet as specified.

To finish

1. Remove the tape from all edges of the Aida cloth.
2. Place the work face down on a padded ironing board and steam press.
3. Center the cardboard backing on the back of the cross stitch and tape the edges of the fabric down.
4. Pull the fabric so it is taut, checking the front to be sure the picture is not distorted. (See p. xiii for framing directions.)
5. Place the finished work in the frame and hang.

VEGETABLE SAMPLER

Each square equals 1 stitch

Color key	DMC #
Orange	740
Pink	602
Dark Brown	938
Light Green	704
Dark Green	700
Olive	3013
Red	349
Blue	826
Outline on carrot and pumpkin—Dark Brown	938

Orange Pink Light Green Dark Green Olive Red

SUMMER SCENE PILLOW

Create this summer scene on a blue background and turn it into a pillow or frame it to hang. It makes a nice hospitality gift for someone who has invited you to a summer house, or it can be tucked into a favorite bedroom chair. The finished pillow is 11 × 14 inches and the cross stitch area is 8 × 11 inches. Use a fabric to match your decor when making the ruffle.

Materials

14-count blue Aida cloth, 8½ × 11½ inches
embroidery floss in colors indicated on chart
needle
hoop
1½ yards of ½-inch-wide eyelet
strip of fabric 2 × 45 inches (can be pieced)
fabric for backing
polyester stuffing
masking tape

Directions

1. Begin by binding all raw edges of the Aida cloth with masking tape.
2. Using the charted design provided, find the center square, which is solid.
3. Count the number of squares up and out from that point to the beginning of the first line of the charted design.
4. Find the center of the fabric by folding it in half vertically, then horizontally.
5. Each square on the graph corresponds to a square on your fabric. Since they are not always the same size, you count but do not measure.
6. Find your starting point for the first stitch.

To work the stitches

1. Separate the strands of embroidery floss.
2. Rejoin three strands of white floss, approximately 18 inches long, and thread your needle. Normally you would use two strands of floss with 14-count Aida, but since the floss is worked on a darker background, you will use three strands throughout.
3. With the Aida secured in the embroidery hoop, begin stitching according to the chart.
4. When finished, remove tape from all edges and place the work face down on a padded ironing board. Steam press.

To assemble pillow top

1. With right sides facing and raw edges aligned, pin the eyelet around the outside edges of the stitched Aida. Machine stitch together with a ¼-inch seam allowance.

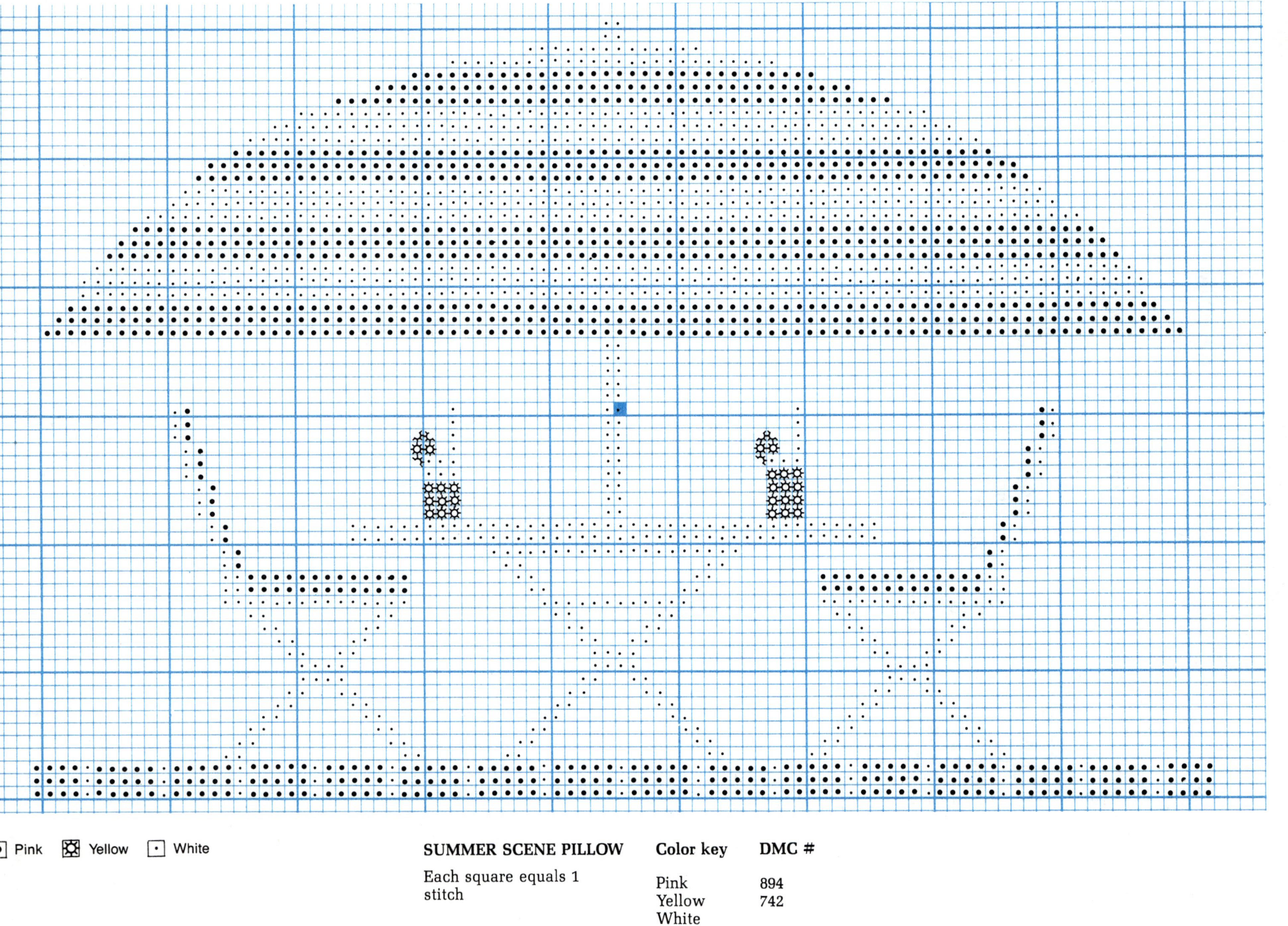

SUMMER SCENE PILLOW

Each square equals 1 stitch

Color key	DMC #
Pink	894
Yellow	742
White	

2. Turn one long edge of the fabric strip under 1/4 inch and press. Turn under another 1/4 inch and press. Stitch the hem.
3. With right sides facing and raw edges aligned, stitch together the two short ends of the strip to form a loop.
4. Divide the fabric into four equal parts and mark each with a pin.
5. With right sides facing and raw edges aligned, gather the fabric as you pin it between these points from corner to corner around the pillow top.
6. Using a 1/4-inch seam allowance, stitch the ruffle to the pillow top all around.

To finish pillow

1. Cut a piece of backing fabric the same size as the pillow top and pin together with right sides facing and eyelet and ruffle between.
2. From the wrong side, machine stitch the backing to the pillow, using the ruffle stitches as a guide. Stitch around three sides and four corners.
3. Trim the corners and turn right side out. Press on the wrong side.
4. Stuff pillow, making sure to fill each corner. Slipstitch the opening closed.

CARDINAL PILLOW

This bright red cardinal contrasts nicely with the brown and tan background. This Aida cloth is called Hopscotch and is a product of the Charles Craft Company. It comes 15 × 15 inches in a wide variety of colors. It gives the design a finished border, yet the cross stitch design is worked within the 7-inch square in the center. Brown piping is used around the outside to finish the pillow with a tailored look, and muslin is used for the backing. The finished pillow is 14 × 14 inches.

Materials

14-count brown Hopscotch Aida cloth, 15 × 15 inches
embroidery floss in colors indicated on chart
needle
hoop
1 3/4 yards of brown piping
muslin, 14 1/2 × 14 1/2 inches
polyester stuffing or 14-inch pillow form
masking tape

Directions

1. Begin by binding all raw edges of the Aida cloth with masking tape.
2. Using the charted design provided, find the center square, which is solid.
3. Count the number of squares up and out from that point to the beginning of the first line of the charted design.
4. Find the center of your fabric by folding it in half vertically, then horizontally.
5. Each square on the graph corresponds to a square on your fabric. Since they are not always the same size, you count but do not measure.
6. Find your starting point for the first stitch. This might be the tip of the green branch, or move down and out to begin from the cardinal's tail.

To work the stitches

1. Separate the strands of embroidery floss.
2. Rejoin two strands of floss, approximately 18 inches long, and thread your needle.
3. Follow the chart to determine where each stitch in each color is placed. Some stitchers prefer working all the stitches in one color before changing to another color. Others like to finish a section of the design, changing colors as needed. For this design, either method is practical.
4. Stop to check your place every so often, and if you're working all the same color stitches before changing colors, recount for placement each time you move to a new section of the design.
5. Remove tape from the edges after the work is finished. Place the cross stitch face down on a padded ironing board and steam press.

To assemble pillow top

1. The pillow top measures 15 × 15 inches; however, to make the pillow 14 × 14 inches, I trimmed away 1/2 inch all around, leaving 1/2 inch for seam allowance. This is a better proportion to go with the design and will fit a standard pillow form.

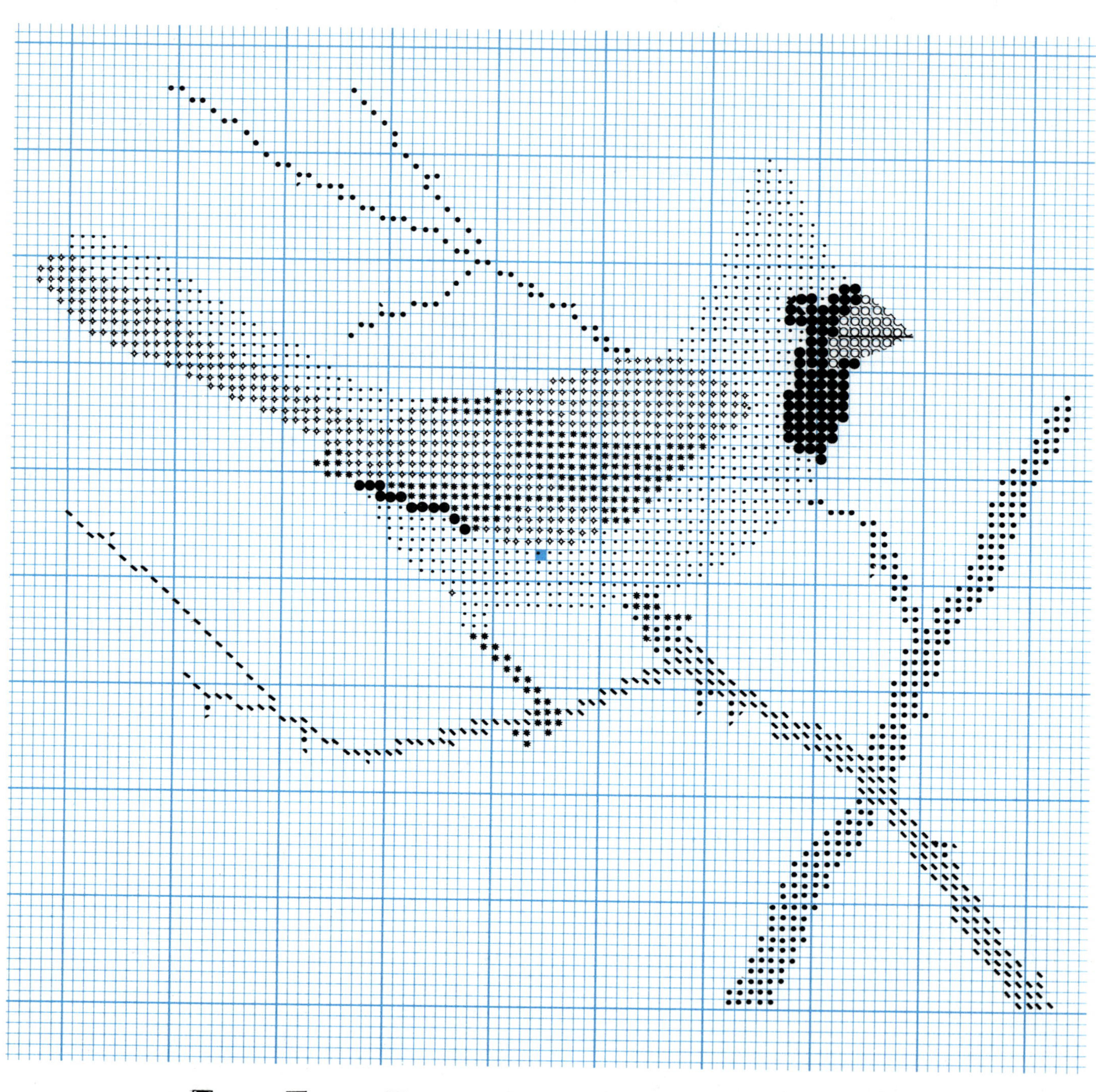

CARDINAL PILLOW

Color key	DMC #
Black	
Yellow	742
Maroon	814
Red	666
Brown	920
Olive	3011
Light Olive	3013

Each square equals 1 stitch

2. With right sides facing and raw edges aligned, pin the piping around the edges of the pillow top.
3. Machine stitch as close to the cording as possible (use a zipper foot on your machine if possible).

To finish pillow

1. With right sides facing and raw edges aligned, pin the muslin backing piece to the pillow top.
2. Stitch all around three sides and four corners, leaving a few inches open for turning.
3. Clip corners and trim excess seam allowance as close to the stitch line as possible.
4. Turn right side out and press the wrong side of the pillow.
5. Fill with stuffing or a pillow form, making sure to fill each corner sufficiently.
6. Slipstitch the opening closed.

WILD DUCK SCENE

This duck scene is created against a light gray Aida cloth background. The ducks are black, brown and white, and when framed in a dark brown wooden frame, this scene makes a handsome addition to a den wall. It is a clean, simple design and one that is easy to work. Whether framed or made into a pillow, this is a nice gift for Dad. The finished cross stitch is 8 × 10 inches.

Materials

14-count gray Aida cloth, 10 × 12 inches
embroidery floss in colors indicated on chart
needle
hoop
10 × 12–inch frame
masking tape

Directions

1. Begin by taping edges of the Aida cloth with masking tape.
2. Using the charted design provided, find the center square, which is solid.
3. Count the number of squares up and out from that point to the beginning of the first line of the design.
4. Find the center of the fabric by folding it in half vertically, then horizontally.
5. Each square on the graph corresponds to a square on your fabric. Since they are not always the same size, you count but do not measure.
6. Find the starting point for the first stitch. You can either finish one duck and then move on to the next, or work all stitches in the same color before changing to the next color.

To work the stitches

1. Separate the strands of embroidery floss.
2. Rejoin two strands of black floss, approximately 18 inches long, and thread your needle.
3. Follow the chart to determine where each stitch in each color is placed. When working the white stitches, use three strands of floss rather than two.
4. When finished, remove the tape from all edges of the Aida and place the work face down on a padded ironing board. Steam press.

To finish

1. With the cross stitch picture face down, center the frame backing on the cloth.
2. Pull the extra Aida cloth to the back and secure all edges with masking tape. Check the front as you do this to be sure the picture isn't distorted. (See p. xiii for framing details.)
3. You can use a matte board to border the picture, or simply place in a frame as I've done here.

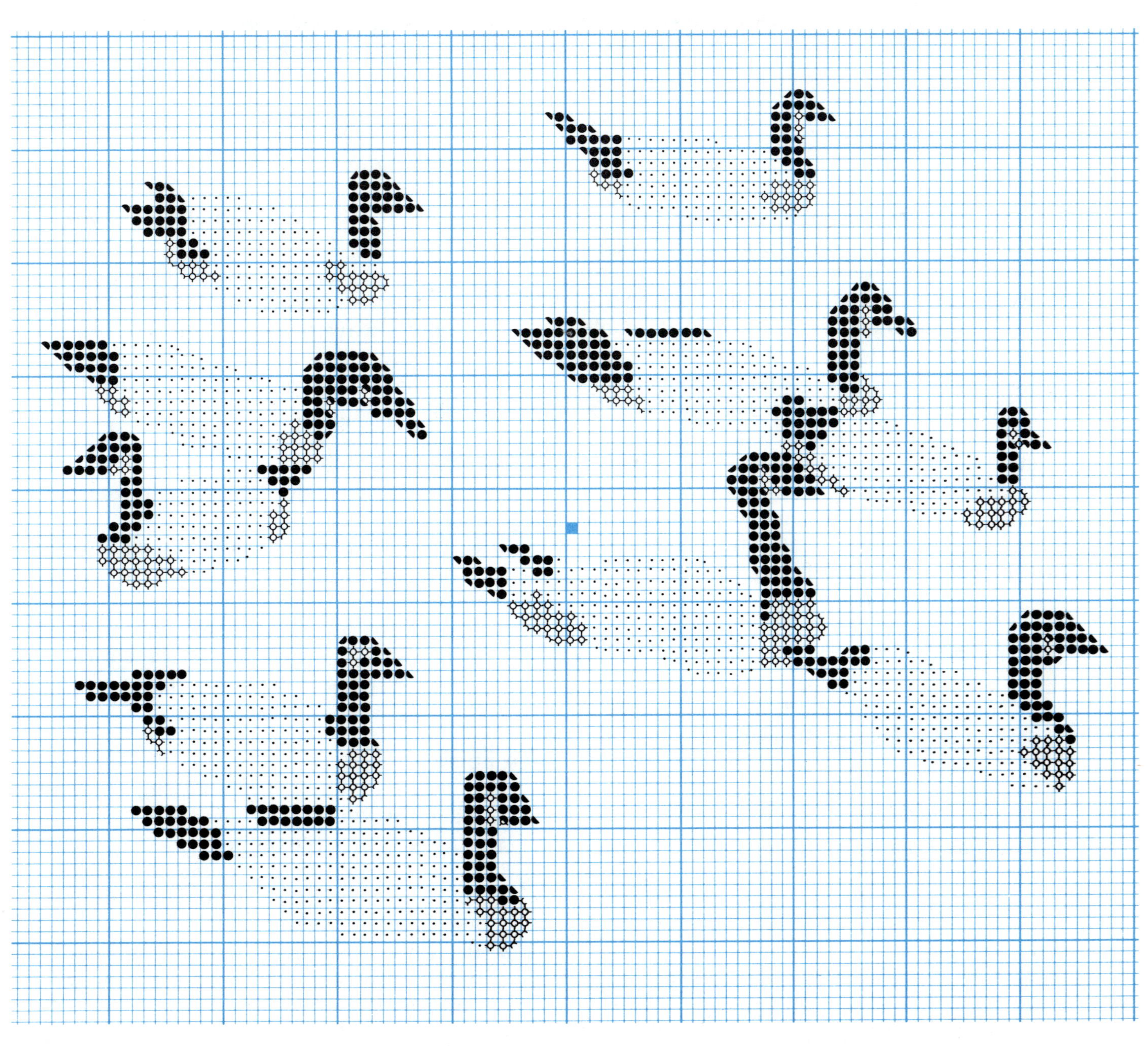

Black Brown White

WILD DUCK SCENE

Color key	DMC #
Black	
Brown	839
White	

Each square equals 1 stitch

HOME SWEET HOME SAMPLER

This is a simple beginner's sampler. It is as nice as any that was created many years ago when this type of embroidery could be found in every home. What makes it a beginner's project is the number of stitches. It won't take you a year to complete, as some samplers often do. While this one looks every bit as lovely as one that is more elaborate, it is always good to know that a project will be completed in a reasonable amount of time. The colors used were selected with care to create an early American country feeling. The finished project is 11 × 14 inches and will fit into a standard frame.

Materials

11-count ecru Aida cloth, 14 × 16 inches
embroidery floss in colors indicated on chart
needle
hoop
frame and matte board
masking tape

Directions

1. Begin by binding all raw edges of the cloth with masking tape.
2. Using the charted design provided, find the center square, which is solid.
3. Count the number of squares up and out from that point to the beginning of the first line of the charted design.
4. Find the center of your fabric by folding it in half vertically and then horizontally.
5. Each square on the graph corresponds to a square on your fabric. Since they are not always the same size, you count but do not measure.
6. Find the starting point for the first stitch of the alphabet.

To work the stitches

1. Separate the strands of embroidery floss.
2. Rejoin three strands of floss, approximately 18 inches long, and thread your needle.
3. Follow the chart to determine where each stitch in each color is placed. Finish the letters and numbers before working on the house area.

To finish

1. Remove the tape from all edges and place the work face down on a padded ironing board. Steam press.
2. Trim the Aida cloth around the design so it fits your frame. (See p. xiii for framing directions.)
3. Place the work over the backing board of the frame and center the matte board and frame over it.
4. Place in the frame and hang.

HOME SWEET HOME SAMPLER	Color key	DMC #
Each square equals 1 stitch	Brown	898
	Rust	919
	Mustard	725
	Blue	312
	Green	989
	Black	

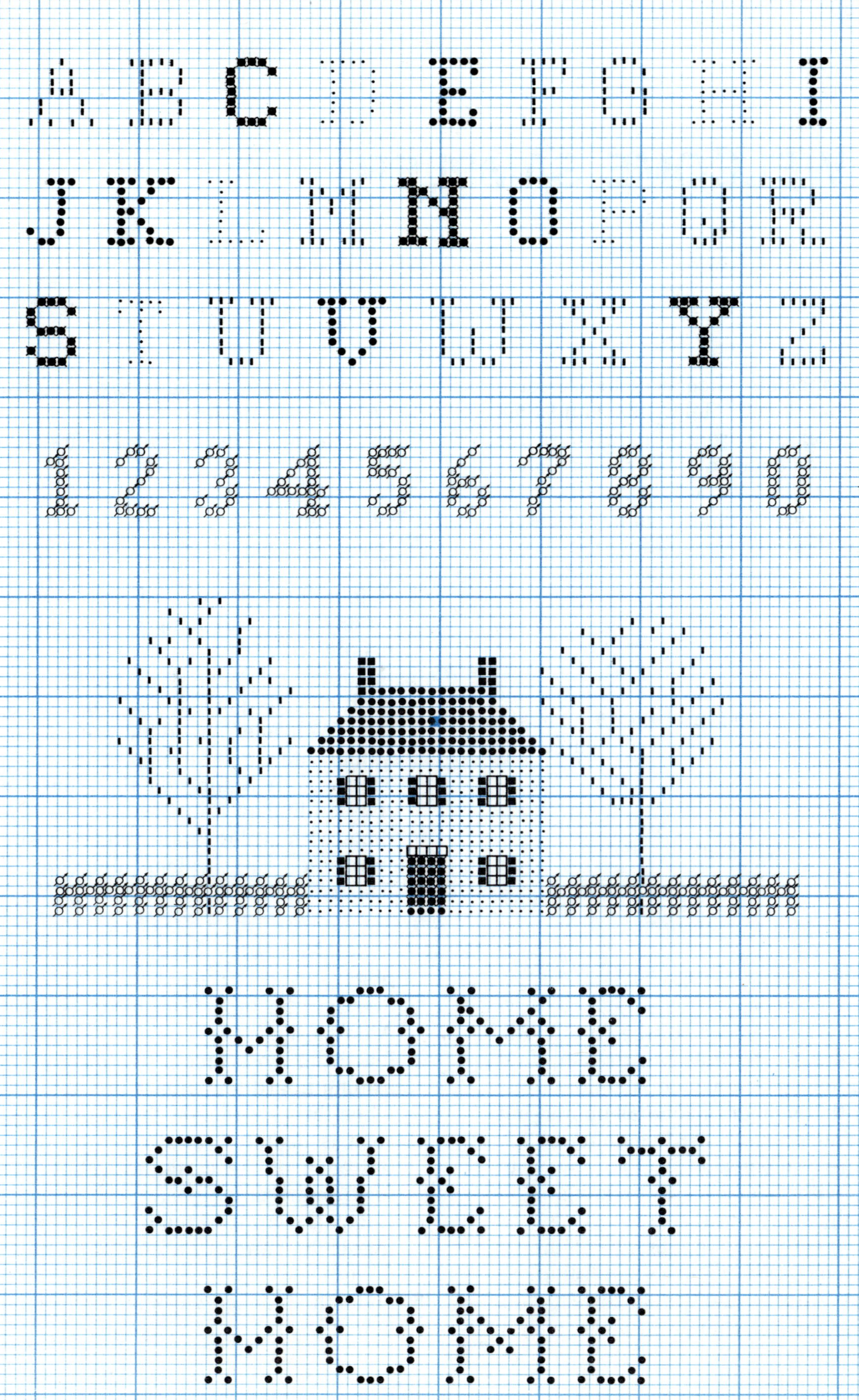

- Rust
- Brown
- Mustard
- Blue
- Green
- Black

WELCOME SAMPLER

This is an especially nice way to welcome guests to your home. Hang this handsome framed sampler in a front hallway area for guaranteed compliments. The finished framed project is 12½ × 16½ inches. The dark wood frame and the brown matte create a dramatic border surrounding the cross stitch done on ecru Aida cloth.

Materials

11-count ecru Aida cloth, 10 × 14 inches
embroidery floss in colors indicated on chart
needle
hoop
frame and matte board
masking tape

Directions

1. Begin by taping edges of the Aida cloth.
2. Using the charted design provided, find the center square, which is solid.
3. Count the number of squares up and out from that point to the beginning of the first line of the design. You may want to begin with the row of buildings and leave the word until last.
4. Find the center of the fabric by folding it in half vertically, then horizontally.
5. Each square on the graph corresponds to a square on your fabric. Since they are not always the same size, you count but do not measure.
6. Find the starting point for the first stitch.

To work the stitches

1. Separate the strands of embroidery floss.
2. Rejoin three strands of floss, approximately 18 inches long, and thread your needle.
3. Follow the chart to determine where each color is placed. The solid lines on the "Welcome" are done with a backstitch with three strands of black floss. There is an outline on the church and red building as well. The flagpole is also done with a black backstitch. These are indicated by straight lines on the charted design.

To finish

1. Remove the tape from all edges of the Aida cloth.
2. Place the work face down on a padded ironing board and steam press.
3. Place the picture over the frame backing so it is centered, and tape all edges to the back of the cardboard. (See p. xiii for framing directions.)
4. Check the front of the design as you do this to be sure you aren't distorting the picture.
5. Place the finished work in the frame and hang.

WELCOME SAMPLER

Each square equals 1 stitch

Color key	DMC #
Blue	798
Light Blue	827
Red	817
Green	988
Brown	919
Light Brown	921
Black	
Grey	415
Outline—Black	

PLATE 13 *"I'm Dreaming of a White Christmas," Christmas Card Cut-outs*

PLATE 14 "Joy" Pillow, Happy Holiday Cards

PLATE 15 Christmas Ornaments, "Joy" Door Hanger

PLATE 16   Friendship Plaques, Wedding Plaque

PLATE 17 Anniversary Plaque, Photo Album

Book Three

First Steps in Counted Cross Stitch

Special Occasions

"JOY" PILLOW

Spread cheer throughout the house at Christmastime with this pillow that says it all. Measuring 9 × 9 inches plus a 2-inch-wide eyelet ruffle, this little pillow can be added to the other pillows on your couch or placed in a holiday basket at your front doorway. If given as a gift, it will surely be enjoyed over and over again each year.

Materials

14-count white Aida cloth, 10 × 10 inches
embroidery floss in colors indicated on chart
needle
hoop
package of 1½-inch-wide craft ribbon
package of narrow piping
30 inches of 2-inch-wide eyelet
fabric for backing (Christmas print)
polyester stuffing
masking tape

Directions

1. Begin by binding all raw edges of the cloth with masking tape.
2. Using the charted design provided, find the center square, which is solid.
3. Count the number of squares up and out from this point to the beginning of the first line of the charted design.
4. Find the center of your fabric by folding it in half vertically and then horizontally.
5. Each square on the graph corresponds to a square on your fabric. Since they are not always the same size, you count but do not measure.
6. Find the starting point for the first stitch of the "J." To be sure that your spacing is perfect, first work each "J" in each row, followed by the wreaths and finally all the "Y's."

To work the stitches

1. Separate the strands of embroidery floss.
2. Rejoin two strands of floss, approximately 18 inches long, and thread your needle.
3. Follow the chart to determine where each stitch in each color is placed.
4. When finished, remove the tape from all edges and place the work face down on a padded ironing board. Steam press.

To assemble pillow top

1. With right sides facing and raw edges aligned, stitch a strip of craft ribbon to each side of the pillow top. Open and press.
2. With right sides facing and raw edges aligned, stitch the piping to the outer edge of the craft ribbon all around.
3. Repeat with the eyelet ruffle all around, machine stitching from the wrong side in

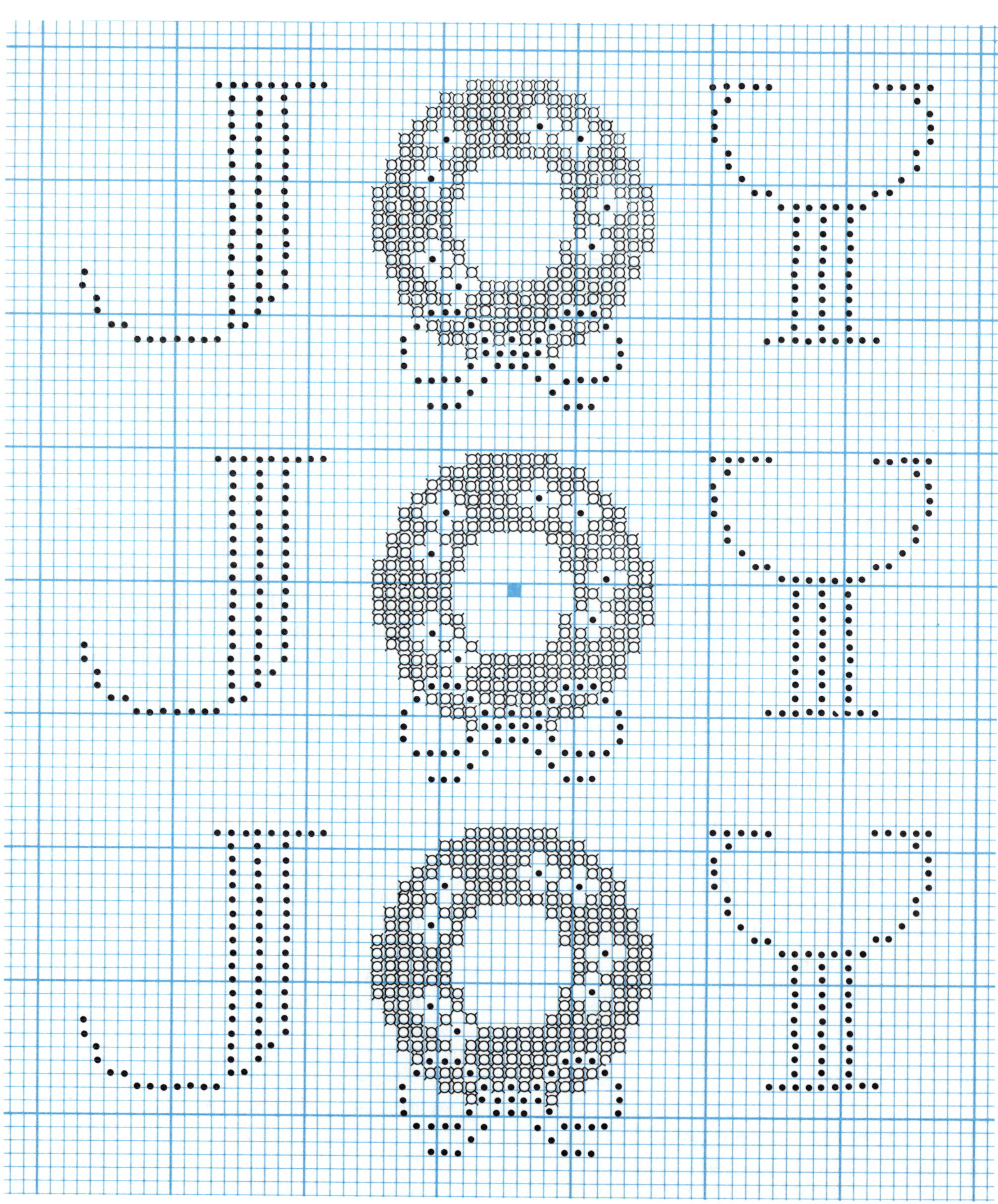

⌼	Green
●	Red

"JOY" PILLOW

Color key	**DMC #**
Red	666
Green	911

Each square equals 1 stitch

order to use the piping stitches as a guide.

To finish pillow

1. With right sides facing and raw edges aligned, pin the backing fabric to the pillow top. The ruffles, ribbon and piping are between.
2. From the wrong side, machine stitch the backing to the pillow, using the ruffle stitches as a guide. Stitch around three sides and four corners.
3. Trim the corners and turn the pillow right side out. Press from the back side.
4. Stuff the pillow and slipstitch the opening closed.

"JOY" DOOR HANGER

Greet your guests with a door hanger that celebrates the Christmas season. It's easy to make, and you can use the alphabet for many other projects. For example, make personalized coasters or a hanging banner. You might prefer the word "Cheers" or "Noel." The finished project is 3 × 11 inches.

Materials

14-count white Aida cloth, 6 × 16 inches
embroidery floss in colors indicated on chart
needle
hoop
rickrack or ribbon for trim
one side fusible interfacing
masking tape

Directions

1. Begin by taping the edges of the Aida cloth.
2. Using the charted design provided, find the center square, which is solid.
3. Count the number of squares up and out from that point to the beginning of the first line of the design.
4. Leave approximately 3 inches of fabric above your starting stitch at the top of the "J" for cutting out the circle.
5. Each square on the graph corresponds to a square on your fabric.

To work the stitches

1. Separate the strands of embroidery floss.
2. Rejoin two strands of floss, approximately 18 inches long, and thread your needle.
3. Follow the chart to determine where each color is placed.
4. When all cross stitch is finished, remove the tape from the edges and place the work face down on a padded ironing board. Steam press.

To finish

1. Trace the pattern from the book. This represents the top half of the door hanger. Turn the tracing around and trace the bottom half of the shape.
2. Center the tracing over your Aida cloth so that the hole to be cut out is approximately 8 rows above the first stitch of the berry over the "J."
3. Pin the pattern to the fabric and cut out the shape. Cut out the hole for the doorknob.
4. Cut a corresponding shape from fusible web interfacing.
5. Fuse the interfacing to the back of the finished cross stitch with a medium hot iron.
6. Stitch or glue the rickrack trim around all raw edges of the door hanger.

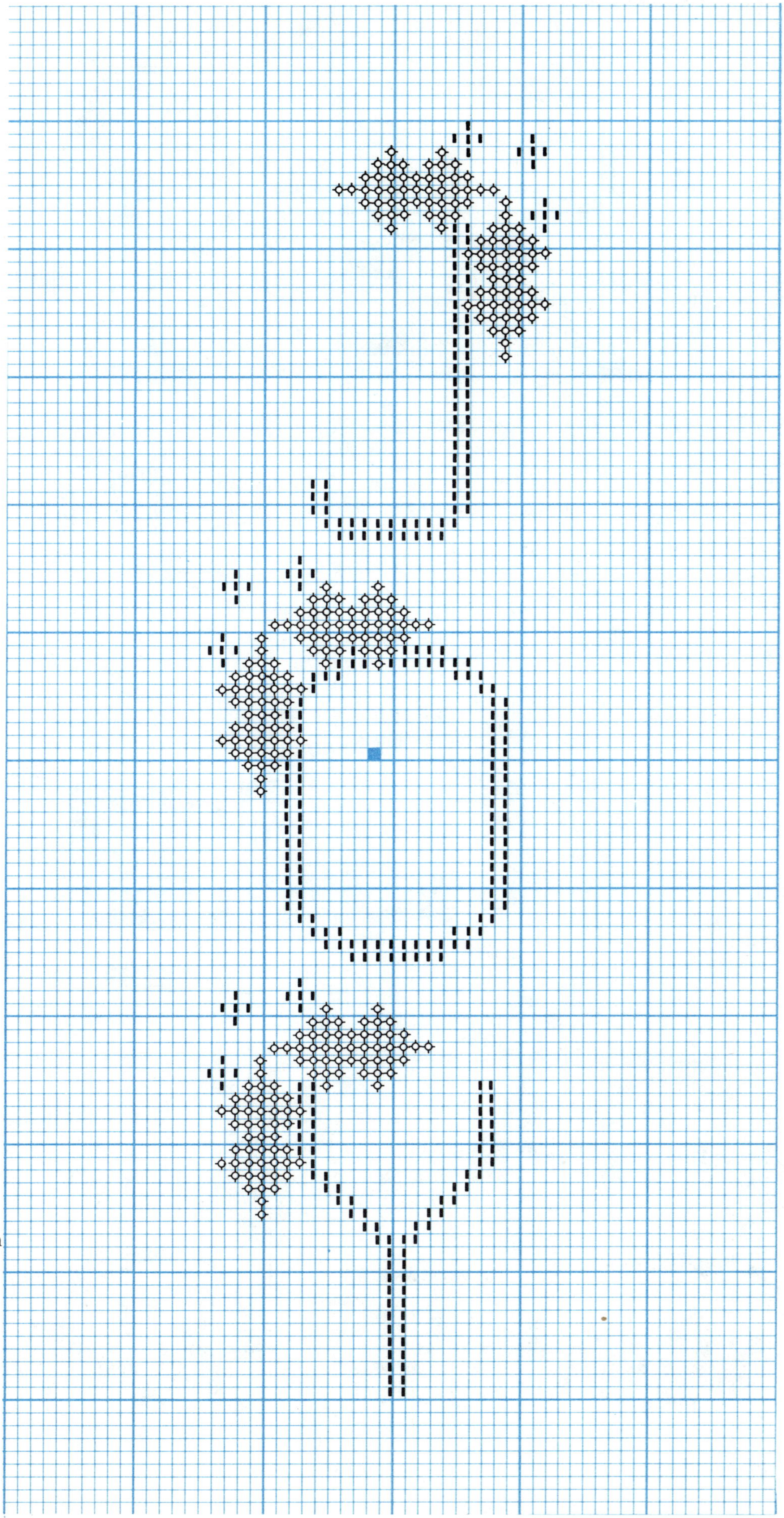

"JOY" DOOR HANGER

Color key	DMC #
Red	666
Green	911

Each square equals 1 stitch

Green

Red

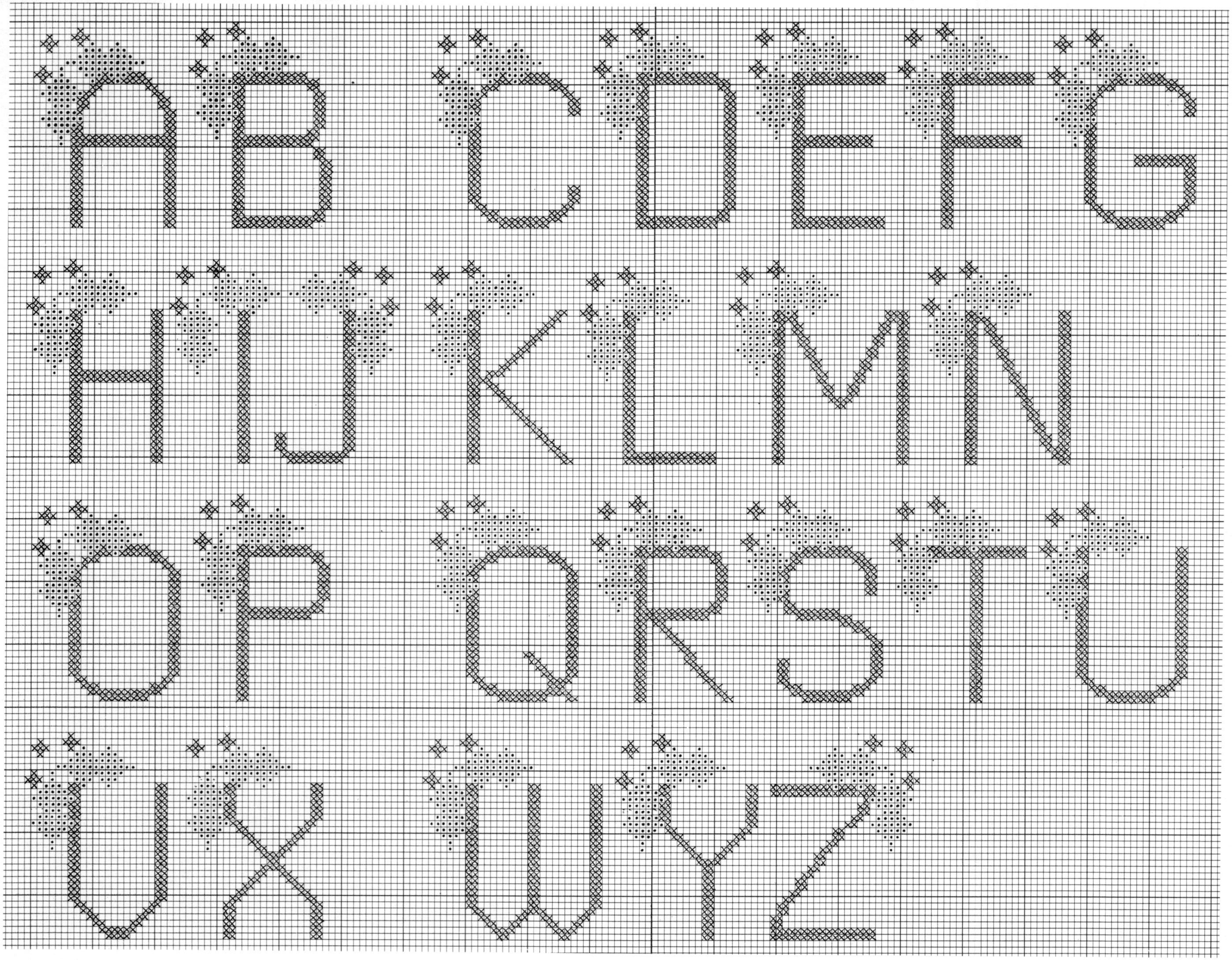

You can substitute your own favorite holiday message for "Joy." Use this letter chart as a guide

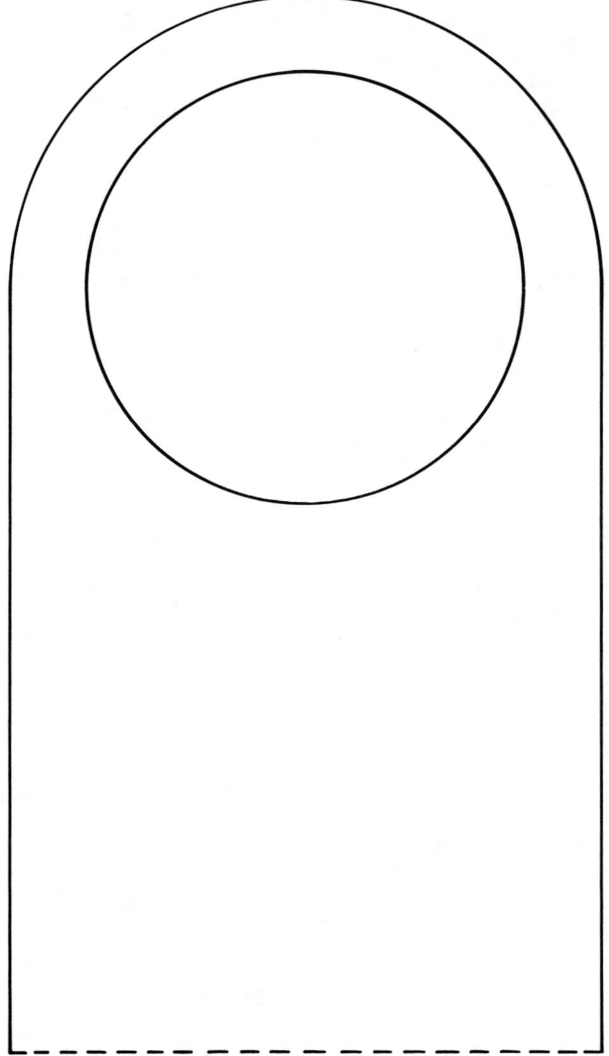

Pattern for "Joy" door hanger

POINSETTIA PLACE MAT

At Christmastime it's festive to dress up all areas of your home. You might like to make place mats to use during this period, or make one mat to place on a table. Create a holiday scene on top of the mat, making sure to leave the cross stitched area prominently showing. The band around the mat matches the band around the "Joy" pillow for a coordinated effect. (See p. 3.)

Materials

14-count ecru Aida cloth, 11 × 14 inches
embroidery floss as indicated on chart
needle
hoop
package of 1½-inch-wide craft ribbon
masking tape

Directions

1. Begin by binding all raw edges of the cloth with masking tape.
2. Using the charted design provided, find the center square, which is solid.
3. Determine where you want to place the design on your place mat and count the squares from the edge of the mat to find the starting stitch.
4. Each square on the graph corresponds to a square on your fabric. Since they are not always the same size, you count but do not measure.
5. I have placed the poinsettia design approximately 2 inches down from the top edge and 2 inches in from the right hand edge.

To work the stitches

1. Separate the strands of embroidery floss.
2. Rejoin two strands of floss, approximately 18 inches long, and thread your needle.
3. Follow the chart to determine where each stitch in each color is placed. Begin with the green leaves and stems.

To finish

1. Remove the tape from all edges and place the work face down on a padded ironing board. Steam press.
2. Cut strips of ribbon for each edge of the mat.
3. Fold each strip in half lengthwise and press.
4. Place each ribbon strip over each fabric edge to bind it and machine stitch. Press the mat from the wrong side.

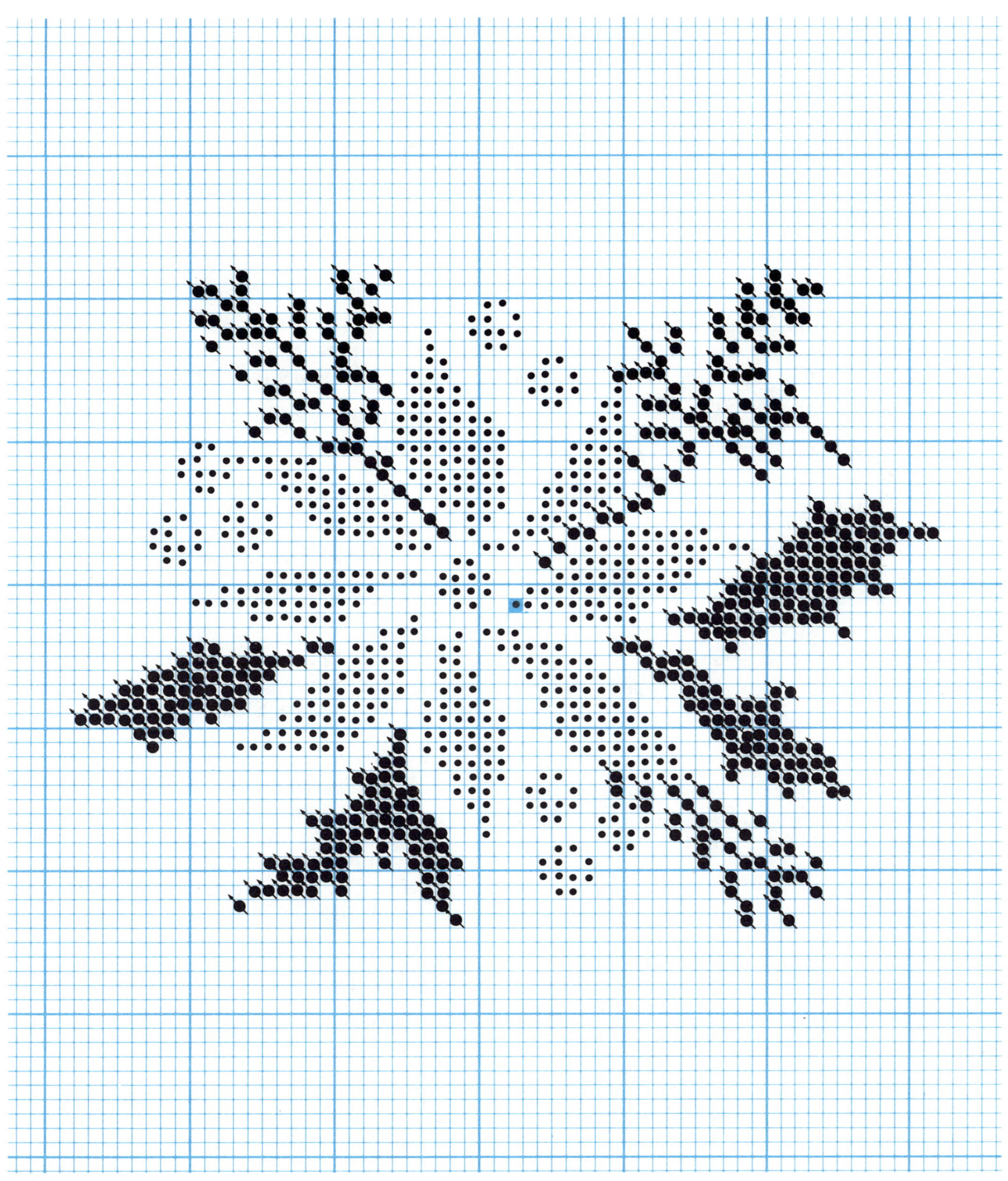

Red

Green

POINSETTIA PLACE MAT

Color key	**DMC #**
Red	666
Green	701

Each square equals 1 stitch

CHRISTMAS ORNAMENTS

This year fill your Christmas tree with handmade cross stitch ornaments. They are easy to make, and you can have fun decorating them with bits of lace, rickrack and ribbons. This is a good way to have a variety of designs inexpensively. They also make terrific bazaar sellers. Nobody can resist their crisp, colorful appeal.

Materials

small pieces of 14-count Aida cloth
embroidery floss in colors indicated on chart
needle
hoop
lace, ribbon, rickrack and eyelet for trimmings
polyester stuffing
masking tape

Directions

1. Use a piece of Aida cloth large enough to fit in a small embroidery hoop. Bind raw edges with masking tape.
2. Using the charted designs provided, find the center square of each design, which is solid.
3. Follow the chart to determine where each stitch for each design will be placed.
4. Each square on the graph corresponds to a square on the fabric. Since they are not always the same size, you count but do not measure.
5. Find the starting point for the first stitch.

To work the stitches

1. Separate the strands of embroidery floss.
2. Rejoin two strands of floss, approximately 18 inches long, and thread your needle.
3. Follow each chart to determine where each stitch of each design will be placed.
4. When finished, remove the tape and place the work face down on a padded ironing board. Steam press.

To make ornaments

1. Cut out each ornament with a 1/2 inch of fabric all around.
2. Cut another piece of Aida cloth or fabric the same size for the backing.
3. If adding lace or eyelet, align raw edges with right sides facing and machine stitch the trim to the front of the ornament.
4. Glue rickrack or ribbon all around. Add bows to corners where desired.
5. Make a ribbon loop and pin the raw end to the center of the top of each with the loop to the front of the cross stitch.
6. Pin the backing to the front of the ornament, with the trim between, and machine stitch, leaving one side open for turning.
7. Trim away excess and clip corners. Turn each one right side out, stuff and slipstitch the opening closed.

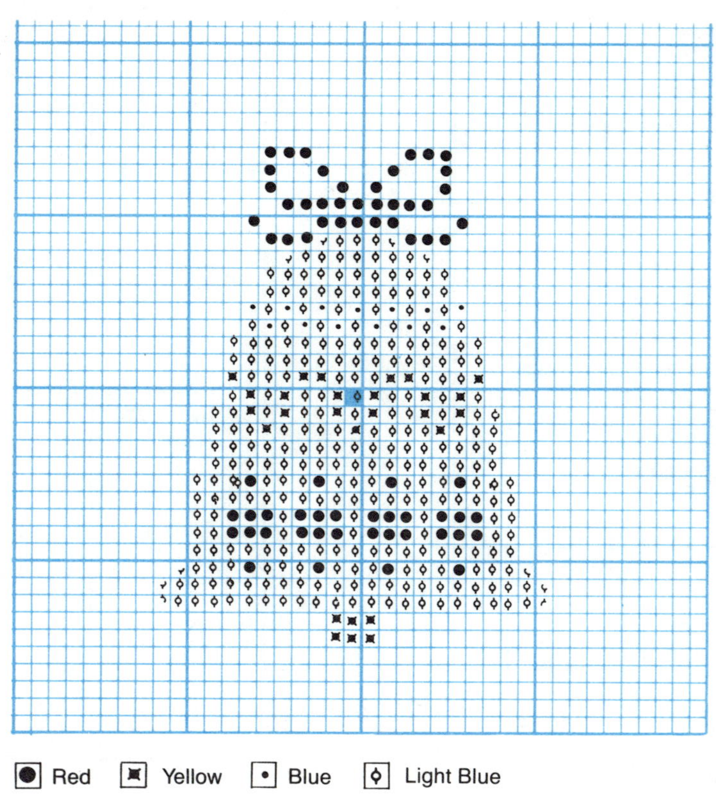

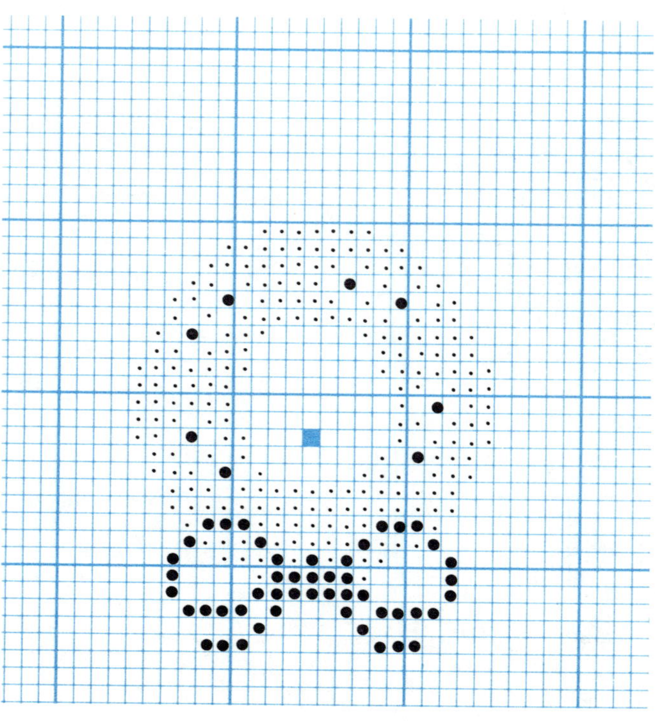

CHRISTMAS ORNAMENTS

Each square equals 1 stitch

Color key	DMC #
Bell	
Red	321
Yellow	307
Blue	797
Light Blue	809
Wreath	
Red	304
Green	911
White	

Red

Color key **DMC #**

Ho Ho Ho
Red 666

Each square equals 1 stitch

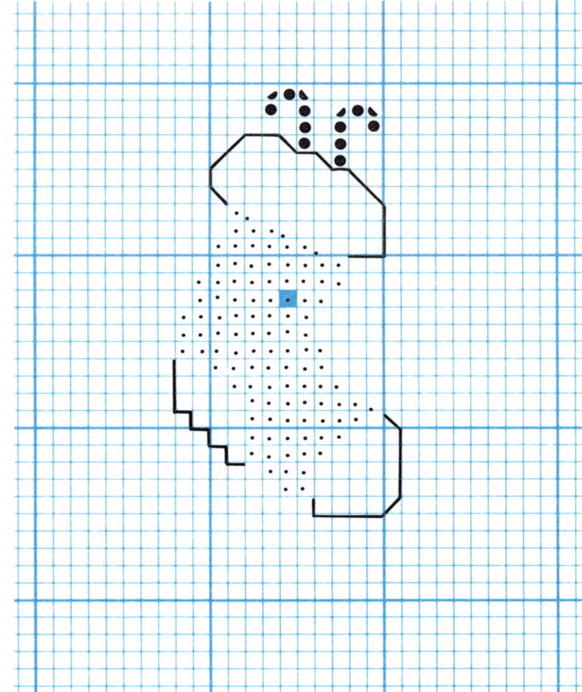

Green Red

Color key **DMC #**

Stocking
Green 911
Red 666

Each square equals 1 stitch

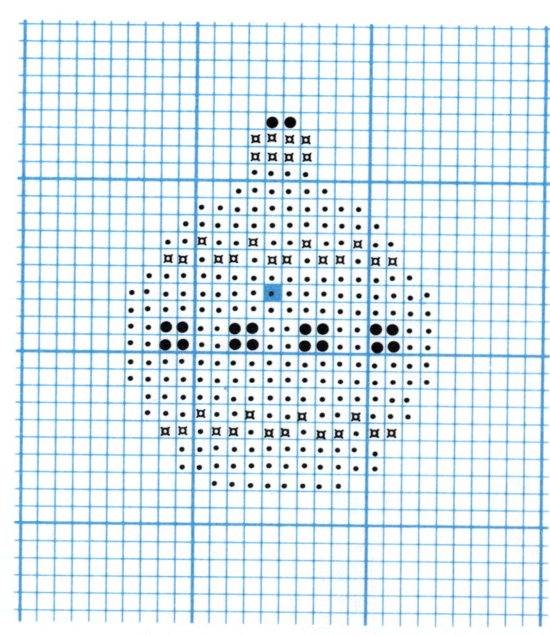

Blue Yellow Red

Color key **DMC #**

Xmas Ball
Blue 322
Yellow 307
Red 321

Each square equals 1 stitch

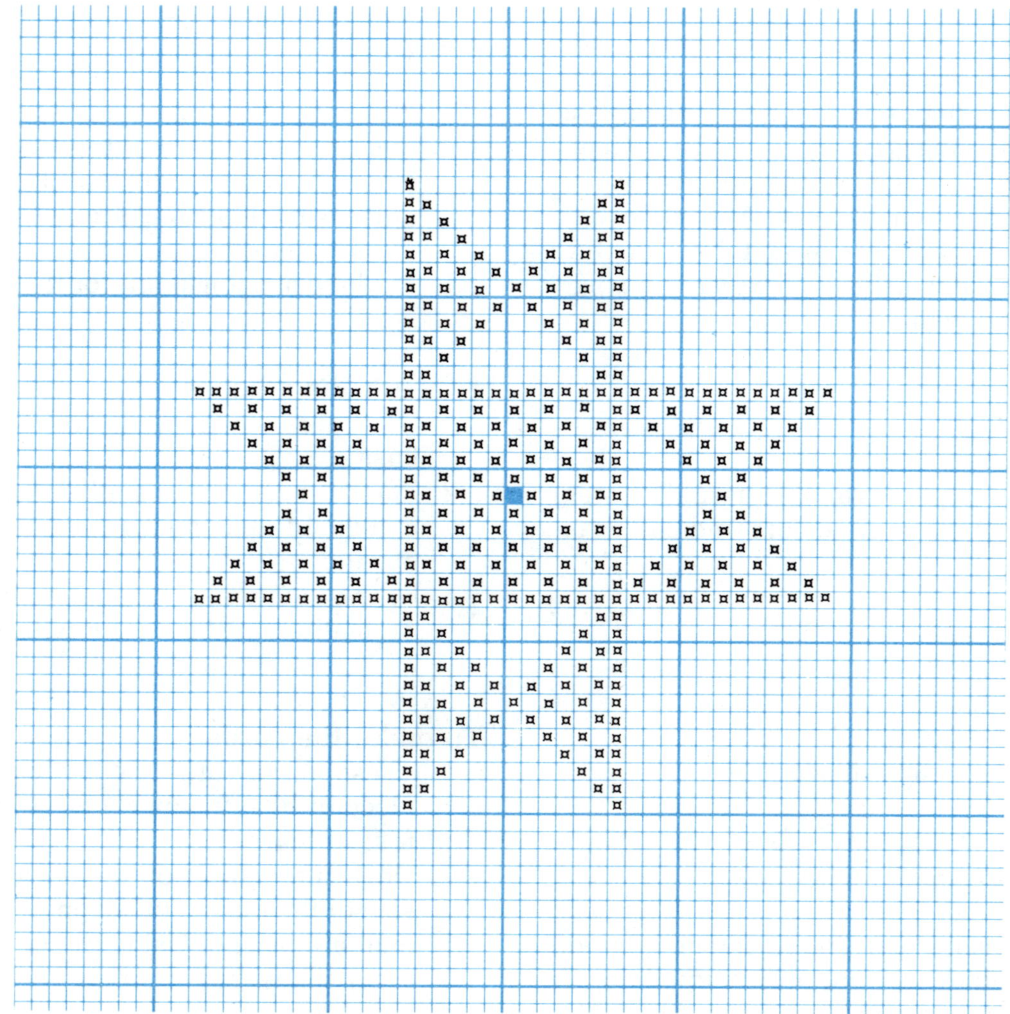

Color key DMC #

Stars
Red 666
White

Each square equals 1 stitch

HAPPY HOLIDAY CARDS

Craft shops carry a perforated paper made especially for cross stitch. It is heavy enough to hold the stitches without ripping and is perfect for making greeting cards. The "Noel" and "Happy Holidays" cards are just an example of what you can do. Almost all the Christmas designs are adaptable for this project. Consider using the paper for small ornaments as well.

Materials

perforated paper (available at craft stores)
embroidery floss in colors indicated on charts
needle
heavy red paper
glue
masking tape
ruler
craft knife or razor blade

Directions

1. When using perforated paper, you do not need to put your project in a hoop or bind the edges.
2. Using the charted designs provided, find the center square of each design, which is solid.
3. Be sure to work on an area of the paper that will allow for enough room around the design for cutting out when finished.
4. Each square on the graph corresponds to a square on the paper. Since they are not always the same size, you count but do not measure.
5. Find the starting point for the first stitch.

To work the stitches

1. Separate the strands of embroidery floss.
2. Rejoin three strands of floss, approximately 18 inches long, and thread your needle.
3. Follow the chart to determine where each stitch of the design will be placed.

To make the cards

1. These cards are 5 × 7 inches. Cut a piece of heavy paper 5 × 14 inches and fold in half.
2. Draw a rectangle on the front that is the size of the design plus approximately 1/4 inch all around. Using the craft knife or razor blade, cut this out.
3. Lift the top flap and glue the corners of the paper design to the underside so that your design shows through the rectangle.

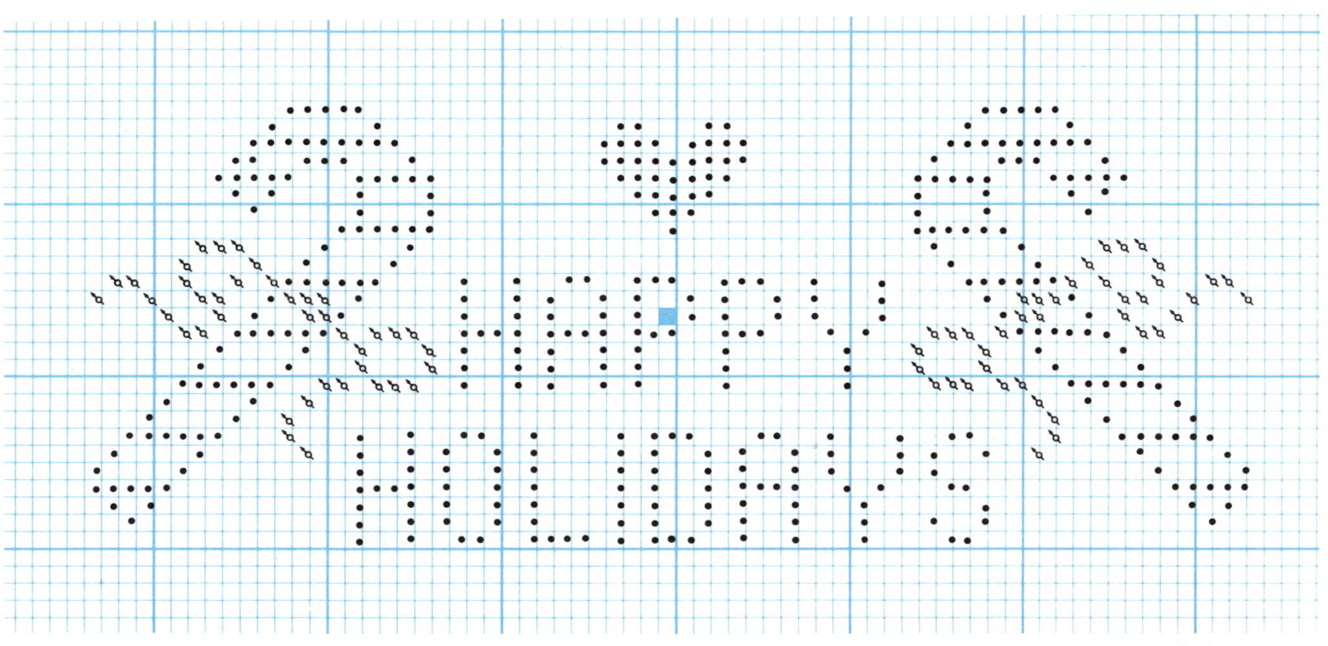

● Red ⍂ Green

HAPPY HOLIDAY CARDS

Each square equals 1 stitch

Color key	DMC #
Happy Holidays	
Red	666
Green	911

Color key	DMC #
Noel	
Green	911
Red	666
Yellow	307
Blue	798
Black	
Pink	605

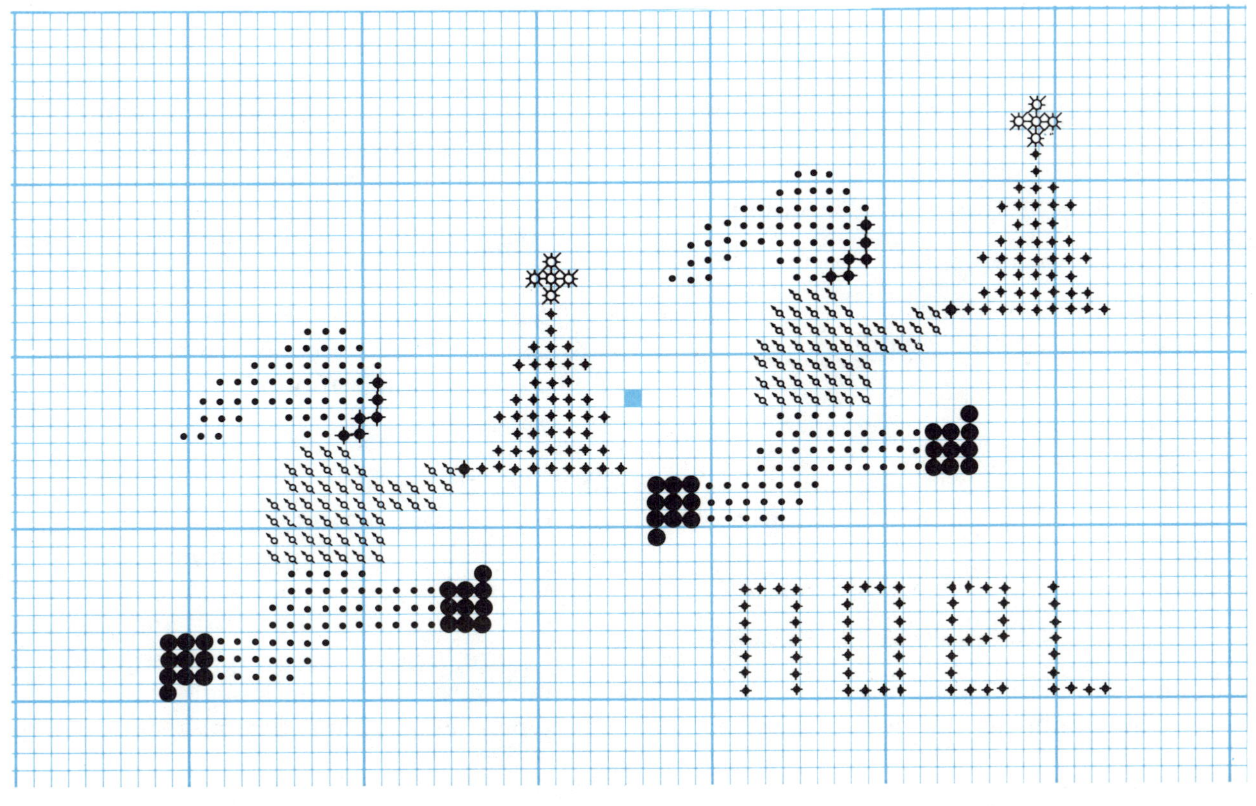

Green Red Yellow Blue Black Pink

CHRISTMAS CARD CUT-OUTS

Small designs are quick and easy to make, so why not whip up a batch of homemade cards this Christmas? There are three different designs that can also be made into little tree ornaments or sachets. Use red, green and white Aida cloth backgrounds. This is a wonderful way to use up the scraps from other projects.

Materials

scrap pieces of 14-count red, green and white Aida cloth
embroidery floss in colors indicated on chart
needle
hoop (small size)
bristol board (heavy paper available at art stores)
white glue
trimmings such as rickrack, ribbon, lace
masking tape
ruler
craft knife or razor blade
marking pens (red and green)

Directions

1. Begin by binding the edges of the Aida cloth with masking tape.
2. Using the charted design provided, find the center square of each design, which is solid.
3. Count the number of squares up and out from that point to the beginning of the first line. You can start at any point on the fabric, as these designs are so small. You may even want to make several on one piece of Aida and then cut each one out. Be sure to leave enough room between each one so there is room for cutting.
4. Each square on the graph corresponds to a square on your fabric.

To work the stitches

1. Separate the strands of embroidery floss.
2. Rejoin two strands of all colors and three strands if you are making the design in white. Cut lengths of floss approximately 18 inches and thread needle.
3. Follow the chart to determine placement of the stitches. Since these designs are all one color, you don't have to change thread.
4. When each design is complete, remove tape and place the work face down on a padded ironing board and steam press.
5. Cut each one out so there is approximately 1/2 inch of fabric around each design.

To make the cards

1. Cut a piece of bristol board 7 × 7 inches for each card and fold in half.
2. Determine the placement of each design on the front of the card and draw a square or rectangle approximately 1/4 inch larger than the design.
3. Open the card out flat on a cutting sur-

face and cut out each drawn area with a craft knife or razor blade.

4. Fold the card as before and spot glue each corner of the design under the cut-out area.

To finish

1. Using the color marker to correspond with the design, write your message on the front of each card.
2. Glue rickrack, ribbons, bells, etc. to the cards.

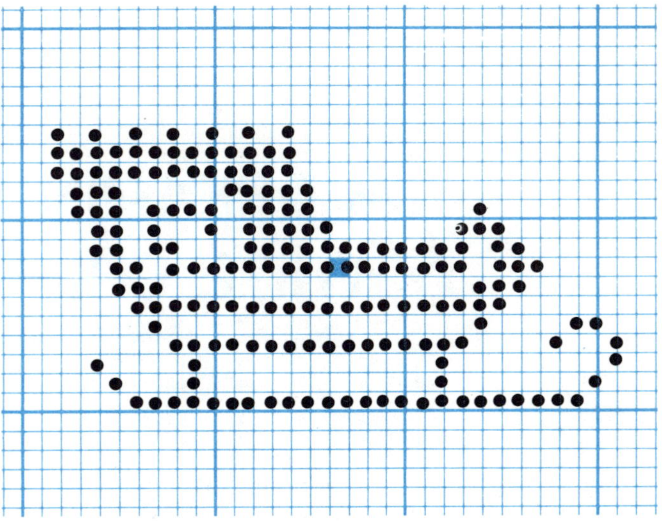

White

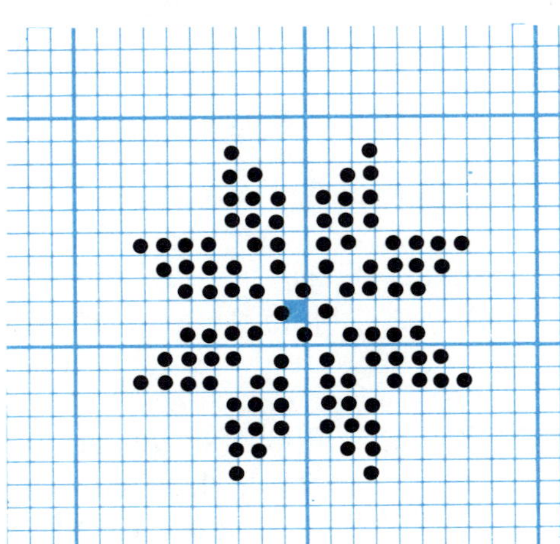

White

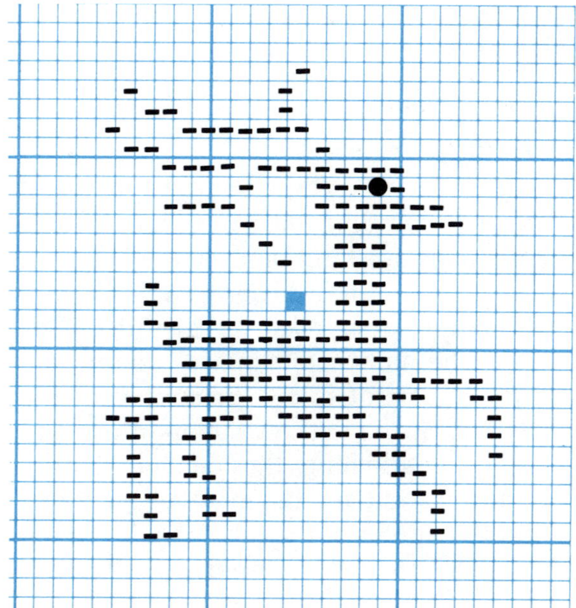

Red

CHRISTMAS CARD CUT-OUTS

Color key	DMC #
White	
Red	321

Each square equals 1 stitch

"I'M DREAMING OF A WHITE CHRISTMAS"

Stitch up this little penguin dreaming of a white Christmas in one evening. It's the perfect last-minute gift for anyone of any age. Who could resist this little character? Surround the finished cross stitch with a bright red matte board to match the penguin's bow tie and add a frame to this 4½ × 8–inch project.

Materials

14-count white Aida cloth, 7 × 11 inches
embroidery floss in colors indicated on chart
needle
hoop
frame and matte board
masking tape

Directions

1. Begin by binding all raw edges of the cloth with masking tape.
2. Using the charted design provided, find the center square, which is solid.
3. Count the number of squares up and out from that point to the beginning of the first line of the design. You may want to begin by stitching the penguin rather than the cloud and saying over his head.
4. Find the center of the fabric by folding it in half vertically, then horizontally.
5. Each square on the graph corresponds to a square on your fabric. Since they are not always the same size, you count but do not measure.
6. Find the starting point for the first stitch. This will be black if you are stitching the penguin first.

To work the stitches

1. Separate the strands of embroidery floss.
2. Rejoin two strands of floss, approximately 18 inches long, and thread your needle.
3. Follow the chart to determine where each stitch of the design will be placed. Since the body of the penguin is white, it is not stitched. This is what makes the project quick and easy. When it is finished, it looks as though, it has all been filled in.

To finish

1. Remove tape from all edges and place the finished work face down on a padded ironing board. Steam press.
2. Trim the Aida cloth, leaving about 1 inch extra all around for wrapping.
3. Center the frame backing on the back of the cross stitch and tape around the edges. Check the front as you do this to be sure it isn't distorted. (See p. xiii for framing directions.)
4. Place matte board over the work and frame.

Blue

Yellow

Red

Black

"I'M DREAMING OF A WHITE CHRISTMAS"

Color key	DMC #
Blue	798
Yellow	742
Red	606
Black	
Letters—Blue	798

Each square equals 1 stitch

ANNIVERSARY PLAQUE

Celebrate a wedding anniversary with this beautiful keepsake. Stitch a floral border, topped with a flowing ribbon bow tie surrounding the couple's name and wedding date. The finished project is 7½ × 9½ inches. When matted and framed, it measures 11 × 14 inches.

Materials

11-count ecru Aida cloth, 10 × 12 inches
embroidery floss in colors indicated on chart
needle
hoop
frame and matte board
masking tape

Directions

1. Begin by taping edges of the Aida cloth with masking tape.
2. Using the charted design provided, find the center square, which is solid.
3. Count the number of squares up and out from that point to the beginning of the first line. You can start with the names and date in the center, or begin with the bow and work down.
4. Find the center of the fabric by folding it in half vertically, then horizontally.
5. Each square on the graph corresponds to a square on your fabric. Since they are not always the same size, you count but do not measure.
6. Find the starting point for the first stitch.

To work the stitches

1. Separate the strands of embroidery floss.
2. Rejoin three strands of floss, approximately 18 inches long, and then thread your needle.
3. Follow the chart to determine where each stitch of the design will be placed.
4. Since the bow and the words are worked in blue floss, you might want to start with these elements, followed by the flowers around the border. In this way the names and date will be perfectly centered.

To finish

1. Remove tape from all edges and place the finished work face down on a padded ironing board. Steam press.
2. Trim the Aida cloth, leaving approximately 1 inch of extra all around.
3. Center the frame backing on the back of the cross stitch and tape around the edges. Check the front as you pull the fabric to be sure it isn't distorted. (See p. xiii for framing directions).
4. Place matte board over the work and frame.

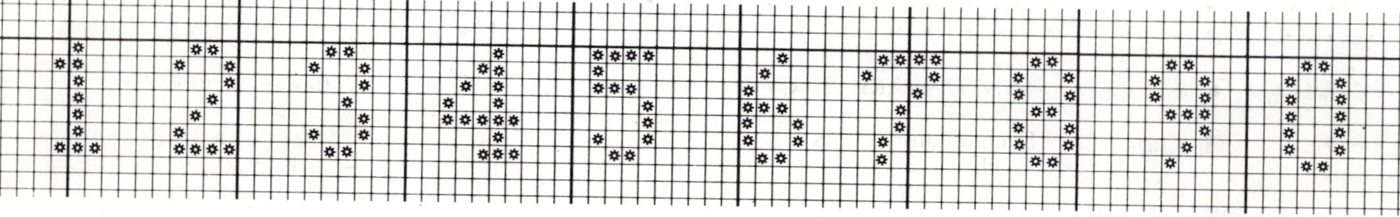

6·16·85

happy 1st anniversary

Dark Pink | Grey
Pink | White

ANNIVERSARY PLAQUE

Each square equals 1 stitch

Color key	**DMC #**
Dark Pink	961
Pink	963
Gray	415
White	

Outline—on border—Dark Pink
"Happy 1st anniversary—Dark Pink
Initials—gray

FRIENDSHIP PLAQUES

Let a friend know how you feel about him or her with a handmade saying plaque. There's always a place on the wall for a pretty framed message. While these projects are framed, you can also make up pillows with the cross stitch in the center, surrounded by a fabric border. "Too much of a good thing" is 3½ × 6½ inches unframed. The "friends" saying is 6 × 9 inches.

Materials

"TOO MUCH": 11-count white Aida cloth, 6 × 9 inches
"FRIENDS": 14-count white Aida cloth, 9 × 12 inches
embroidery floss in colors indicated on charts
needle
hoop
frame and matte board
masking tape

Directions

1. Begin by taping edges of the Aida cloth.
2. Using the charted designs provided, find the center square, which is solid.
3. Count the number of squares up and out from that point to the beginning of the first line of the designs. You may want to begin with the border designs.
4. Find the center of each fabric piece by folding it in half vertically, then horizontally.
5. Each square on the graph corresponds to a square on your fabric. Since they are not always the same size, you count but do not measure.
6. Find the starting point for the first stitch.

To work the stitches

1. For the 11 count, you will use three strands of floss. For the 14 count, use two strands. Separate the floss and rejoin the number of strands needed. Cut a length approximately 18 inches and thread your needle.
2. Follow the chart to determine where each color will be placed. When stitching a border, check the number of squares and stitches now and then to be sure the spacing is correct.

To finish

1. Remove the tape from all edges of the Aida cloth.
2. Place the work face down on a padded ironing board and steam press.
3. Trim the Aida cloth to within an inch extra all around.
4. Center the backing cardboard on the back of the cross stitch and tape the fabric all around.
5. Check the front of the picture to be sure it isn't distorted. (See p. xiii for framing directions.)
6. Place in frame with matte board and hang.

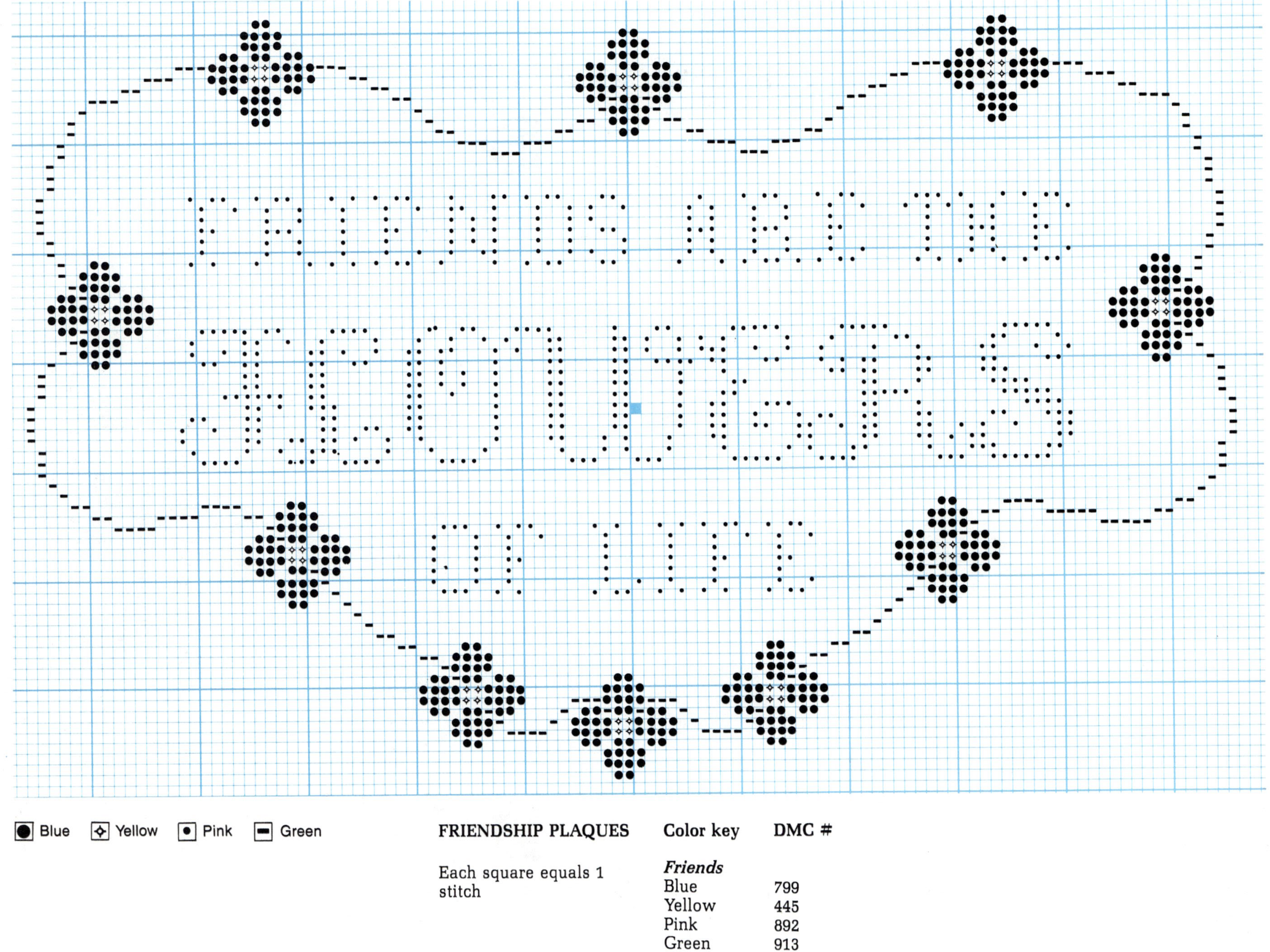

● Blue ✧ Yellow • Pink ▬ Green

FRIENDSHIP PLAQUES

Each square equals 1 stitch

Color key	DMC #
Friends	
Blue	799
Yellow	445
Pink	892
Green	913

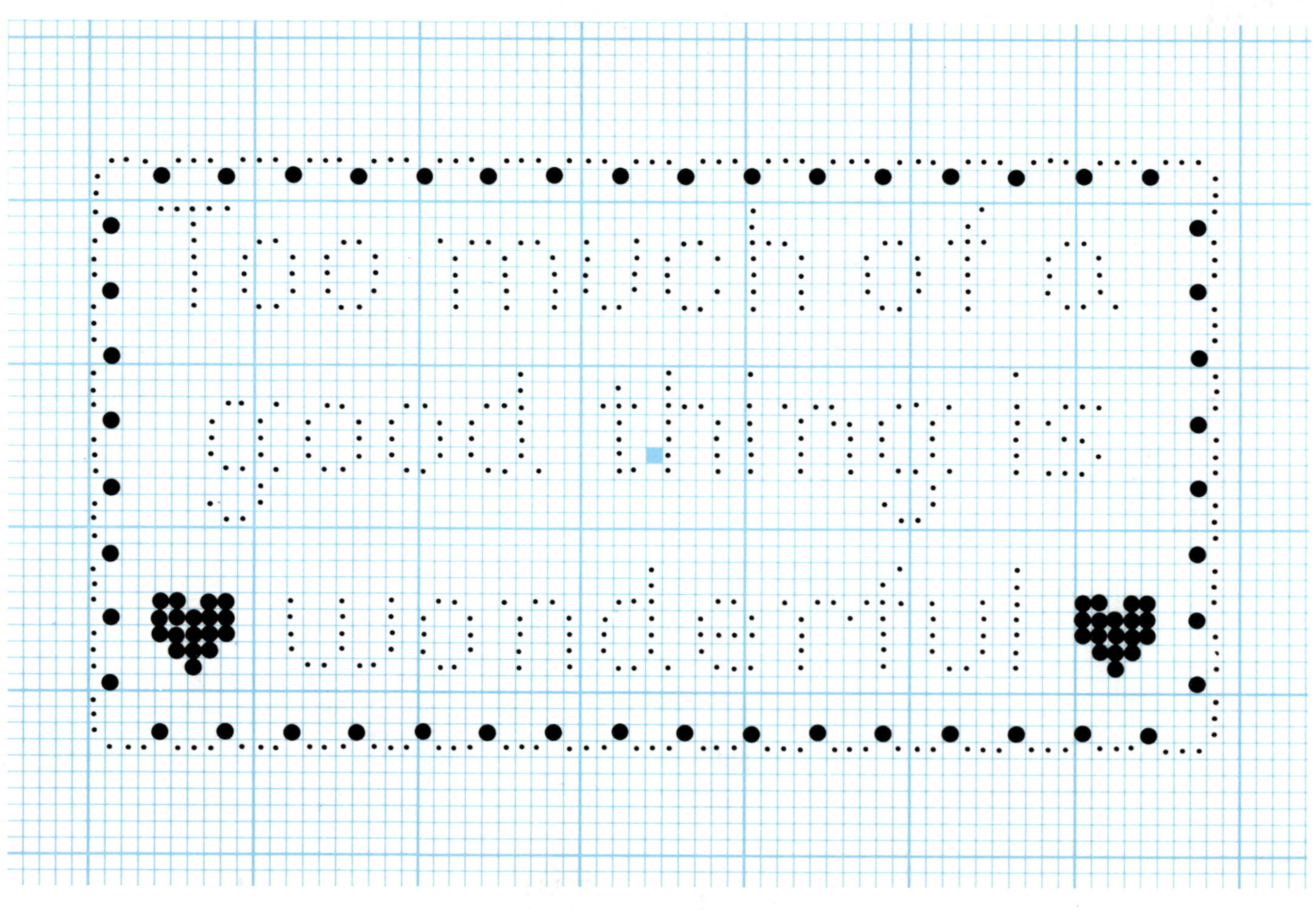

FRIENDSHIP PLAQUES	**Color key**	**DMC #**
Each square equals 1 stitch	*Too much of a good thing*	
	Blue	799
	Red	666

WEDDING PLAQUE

Frame a wedding invitation to give as a gift that will be treasured by the newlyweds. This one was designed by Suzi Peterson and is bordered with a soft gray and bright pink to contrast with the pink Aida cloth background. The finished size is 8 × 10 inches.

Materials

14-count pink Aida cloth, 12 × 14 inches
embroidery floss in colors indicated on chart
needle
hoop
1/8-inch-wide ribbon for bows
frame
masking tape
glue

Directions

1. Begin by taping edges of the Aida cloth with masking tape.
2. Using the charted design provided, find the center square, which is solid.
3. Count the number of squares up and out from that point to the beginning of the first line of the border design.
4. Find the center of your fabric by folding it in half vertically, then horizontally.
5. Each square on the graph corresponds to a square on your fabric. Since they are not always the same size, you count but do not measure.
6. Find the starting point for the first stitch.

Since the border design is placed around the invitation, place your invitation in the middle of the fabric to be sure of the placement of the stitches. Adjust the placement of the border if needed to accommodate your invitation.

To work the stitches

1. Separate the strands of embroidery floss.
2. Rejoin two strands of floss, approximately 18 inches long, and thread your needle.
3. Follow the chart to determine where each color is placed. Stop to count your squares on the chart and fabric now and then to be sure your corners will meet where specified.
4. The wavy lines on each side are created with a backstitch. They are indicated by solid, straight lines on the chart.

To finish

1. Remove the tape from all edges of the Aida cloth.
2. Place the work face down on a padded ironing board and steam press.
3. Trim the excess Aida cloth around the design so it will fit in your frame.
4. Make two small bows and spot glue them on the top and bottom of the invitation.
5. Center the invitation on the Aida background and spot glue it at each corner.
6. Frame and hang or stand on a table. (See p. xiii for framing directions.)

WEDDING PLAQUE

Each square equals 1 stitch

Color key	DMC #	Color key	DMC #
Blue	797	Green	911
Light Blue	813	Yellow	307
Dark Pink	603	Mustard	742
Light Pink	605		

PHOTO ALBUM

There are some very good products made especially for cross stitch designs. One such product is a photo album with a 4 × 6–inch opening on the cover for the insertion of a design. This insert is backed with a foam rubber padding. You simply remove the cloth, work your cross stitch design on your own Aida cloth (in the color and size of your choosing) and reinsert. It makes a nice gift, or keep it for your own family pictures. The initial personalizes the project, and the border adds to the graphic design.

Materials

14-count white Aida cloth, 7 × 8 inches
embroidery floss in colors indicated on chart
needle
hoop
album
masking tape

Directions

1. Begin by taping edges of the Aida cloth with masking tape.
2. Using the charted design provided, find the center square, which is solid.
3. Count the number of squares up and out from that point to the beginning of the first line of the letter you will be cross stitching.
4. Find the center of the fabric by folding it in half vertically, then horizontally.
5. Each square on the graph corresponds to a square on your fabric. Since they are not always the same size, you count but do not measure.
6. Find the starting point for the first stitch. It's best to start with the initial and then work the border. In this way you will know that the letter is perfectly centered.

To work the stitches

1. Separate the strands of embroidery floss.
2. Rejoin two strands of floss, approximately 18 inches long, and then thread your needle.
3. Follow the chart to determine where each stitch of your initial will be placed.
4. When working on the border, check your count from time to time to be sure your corners will be evenly spaced from the center. The perfection of the design depends on perfect centering of the initial within the two borders.

To finish

1. Remove tape from all edges and place the work face down on a padded ironing board. Steam press.
2. Trim the Aida cloth if necessary to fit in the opening space of your album. This project can also be made into an eyeglass case, pillow, sachet or small purse.

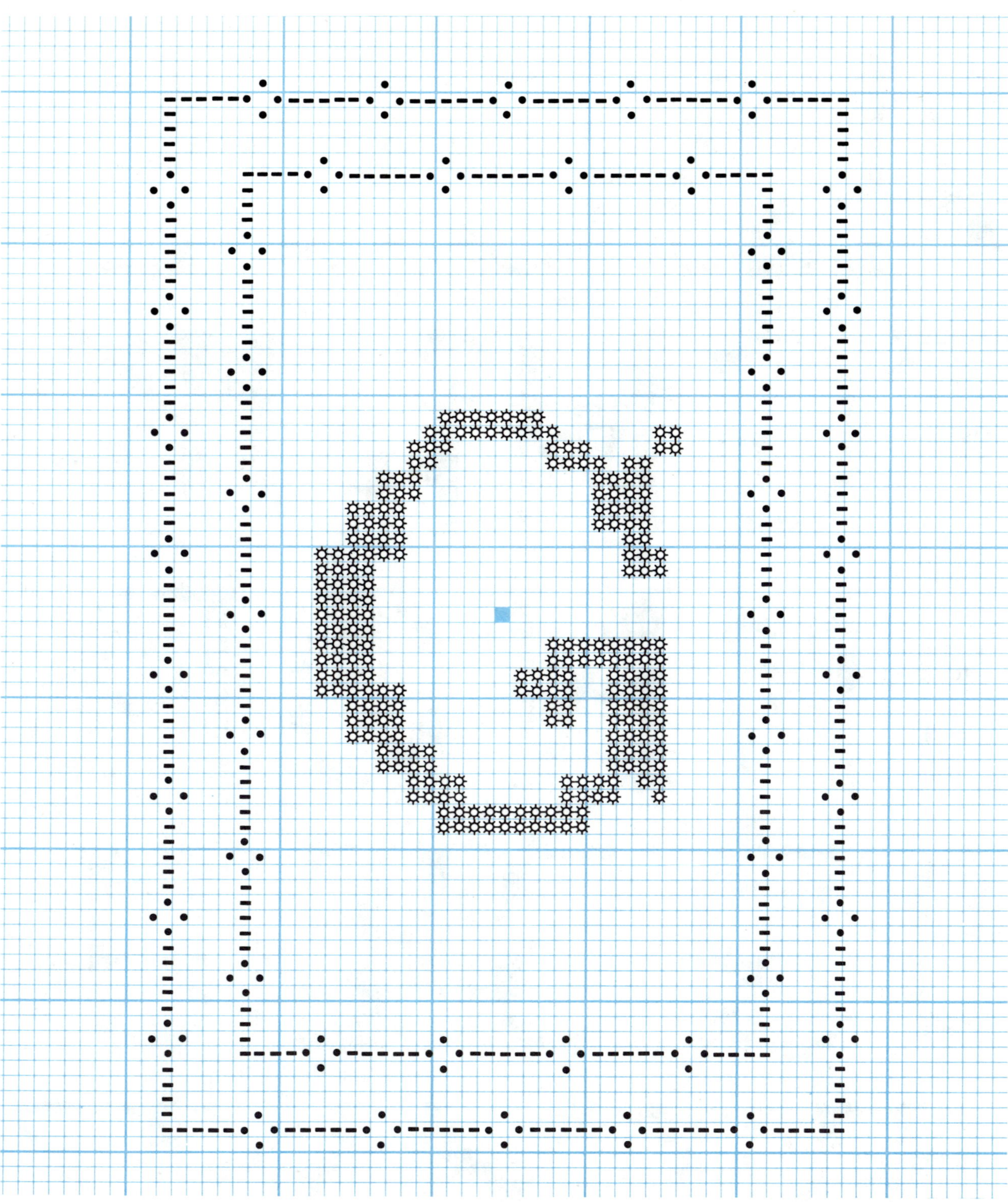

☒ Blue

⊡ Green

⊟ Pink

PHOTO ALBUM

Color key	**DMC #**
Blue	793
Green	704
Pink	605

Each square equals 1 stitch

ABCDE
FGHIJK
LMNOP
QRSTU
VWXYZ